MAKING THE
YOUNG HORSE
THE RATIONAL WAY

MAKING THE
YOUNG HORSE
THE RATIONAL WAY

Elwyn Hartley Edwards

J. A. ALLEN · LONDON

© Elwyn Hartley Edwards
First published in Great Britain 2006

ISBN-10: 0-85131-911-4
ISBN-13: 978-0-85131-911-7

J.A. Allen
Clerkenwell House
Clerkenwell Green
London EC1R 0HT

J.A. Allen is an imprint of Robert Hale Limited

The right of Elwyn Hartley Edwards to be identified as author
of this work has been asserted by him in accordance
with the Copyright, Designs and Patents Act 1988

A catalogue record for this book is available from the British Library

Edited by Martin Diggle
Design and typesetting by Paul Saunders
Illustrations by Maggie Raynor
Photographs by, or property of, the author, except for those on pages
11, 35, 36, 37, 38, 41, 106, 107 (upper), 112, 116, 117, 118, 145, 146 and 209 © Bob Langrish

Colour separation by Tenon & Polert Colour Scanning Limited, Hong Kong
Printed by Midas Printing International Limited, China

Contents

Acknowledgements

My thanks are due to Caroline Burt, formerly Editorial Director of J. A. Allen, for her help and encouragement in the writing of this book and, particularly, to Julie Thomas who has patiently collated and presented my manuscripts over the years and on whose command of modern technology I am entirely reliant.

I have also to thank Maggie Raynor for her illustrations and my editor, Martin Diggle, for his conscientious and painstaking study of the text.

Finally, I owe an ongoing debt of gratitude to my good friend Sian Thomas BHSI who not only organizes horses and equipment for photo shoots but also demonstrates the movements and exercises with such enviable expertise. Without her help this book and others would not have been possible.

Elwyn Hartley Edwards
Chwilog 2005

Introduction

'Riding is a rational science not an instinctive
accomplishment' – and so is the training of the riding horse.

There is no single, definitive method of making a young horse. So much
depends on the intended use. Is he to be a recreational, all-round riding
horse, a harness horse, a racehorse or one bred and schooled specifically for
the more exotic American gaited classes? To a degree the methods employed
rely also on inherited traditions and philosophies. In this respect, it is possible to discern a generalized division between the more formal approach,
largely taken by Europeans concerned with the accepted Olympic disciplines, and that taken by the horse-peoples of the Asian and Eurasian
steppelands and the cowboys of North and South America, the latter, of
course, being the gauchos of the pampas.

The former approach is also adopted by a number of non-European
countries with an interest in international competition, like those of Aust-
ralasia, as well as large parts of the Americas. The latter is more elemental
in character and practice, is accomplished more immediately and inclines
nearer to the rough and ready *breaking* of young animals rather than to the
making of horses who are rationally prepared, physically and mentally, for a
variety of recreational purposes extending over the period of their working
lives.

This book follows the general European pattern and attempts to present a logical sequence of training, a *rational* system, in some detail and spread over distinct periods in the horse's third and fourth years, viewed respectively as primary and secondary education. It is further sub-divided into stages for which I have suggested approximate and certainly flexible time schedules.

The object of the 'rational way' is the production of a versatile riding horse; a rounded individual well able to take part creditably in competitive

The author on the Hungarian Nonius Marcus, with Sian Thomas BHSI on the young Irish Sport Horse, Dr Dolittle.

events at a good middle-of-the-road level, whose preparation allows him to enjoy his working life, while contributing materially to his rider's enjoyment of the relationship.

I am not in favour of the coercive 'gadgets', nor, indeed, of any piece of equipment used coercively, but I recognize that there are certain items of saddlery that are generally available that are used and frequently endorsed by expert horsemen and women.

On that account I have included articles like the Chambon, de Gogue and the Abbot-Davies balancing rein, as well as discussing the much reviled draw- and running-reins; the latter being 'training aids' that have been with us for a good many centuries and are still in evidence today. Under certain conditions and in expert hands they may be permissible, but they can tempt the inexperienced into taking dangerous short cuts.

(Indeed, I have been indulgent by including my own favourite 'gadget', Galvayne's harness, as an example of a piece of equipment that legitimately employs the suggestion of mechanical persuasion to produce a psychological force.)

Conversely, I have not thought it necessary to recommend detailed diet charts appropriate to the different stages of training, since the advanced technology of the horse-feed industry, allied to the expertise of nutritional science, supplies the answers very effectively, and even goes to the trouble of printing them on the bag. Therefore, other than urging the purchase of best quality hay or haylage and the provision of constant fresh water, I have confined myself to reiterating the proven principles of feeding and the proportions relevant to the work being done in the section on Nutrition (in Part 4).

Nonetheless, while appreciating the convenience and value of scientifically balanced feedstuffs and supplements, I have thought it appropriate to remind owners that the well-being of the horse is *their* responsibility, not one to be passed on to the dietician. ('The eye of the master maketh the horse fat' is a good dictum to observe; at least for so long as it is not carried to excess. Obesity in either humans or horses is not to be encouraged. In the first instance, the sufferers cannot touch their toes; in the second the horse is prevented from making directional changes in any semblance of a bend.)

A further example of the influence of scientifically applied technology lies in the renewed 'awareness' of the role of a properly constructed and professionally fitted saddle, as it is relevant to balance, locomotion, and the realization of the potential of both horse and rider. The advance in saddle technology is a landmark in the history of the riding art and is examined at some length in Saddlery and Equipment (Part 2).

Change and progress, even if the latter is not always immediately apparent, are endemic to the human condition, and have unavoidable effects on that of the horse. For example, (other than in Mongolia perhaps) he has changed in physical appearance as a result of selective breeding and improved management techniques, and he continues to do so – the continental Warmbloods are a case in point. There is now a greater divergence in type, a notable improvement in quality and little evidence of the coaching blood that was to be found 20–30 years ago.

The very state of domestication has naturally had its influence on the modern horse, also. He has, willy-nilly, been compelled to place greater reliance for survival on the human agency. In doing so he has become imprinted with superficial characteristics over and above those acquired in the natural state. While the atavistic instincts of the herd animal are never eliminated, it is possible for them to be subdued *a little* by the domestic condition. Horses become more adaptable to human requirements and certainly they are more accepting of human contact; matters which in themselves are a contradiction to the nature of the animal.

Nonetheless, despite these adaptations, we do well to remember that, in basic physiology and structure, the horse is hardly altered by the passing of the centuries. In his essentials, he remains the same as in the beginnings of his domestication by nomadic Eurasian steppe-peoples some 6,000 or more years ago.

Recognition of this situation is an essential factor in dealing with the young horse and it is why two very important sections feature prominently in the first part.

These are an analysis of Essential Anatomy (essential in the sense of relevance to movement, outline, etc.) and a somewhat more expanded study of Nature and Characteristics, and their bearing on training and management.

Without an understanding of both, riding and ownership become beset with problems that are of our own making.

I am well aware that there are methods of training – 'gentling', 'whispering' and so on, that are not described in this book. Usually, they are based on practices that have been with us in one part of the world or another for a very long time. That they may achieve quick results is not necessarily a commendation for their inclusion within the concept of progressive training. I acknowledge, unreservedly, that the best are practised, publicised and demonstrated by skilful horsemasters, possessed of a particular empathy with their equine subjects, as well as a pronounced promotional talent. That

I have personal reservations about the long-term value of some of them is only because, whatever the end-product may be, it does not conform to my requirement for the animal's intended use.

What is described here is simply a logical sequence – a rational way – that is not beyond the competence of the average owner. It does take longer, but it lasts longer, too, and, I believe, it contributes materially to the active, enjoyable working life of what the soldier of World War I regarded appropriately and with real affection as his 'long-faced chum'.

PART 1

Background Considerations

An Overview

The term 'natural horsemanship' has had a particular attraction for horse-lovers every since it first appeared in the nineteenth century or, more accurately, at the turn of that century. The original distinction, now lost, was between classical equitation, based more or less on collection, and the 'natural' system of cross-country riding implemented by the Italian Capt. Federico Caprilli (1868–1907) at the cavalry schools of Tor di Quinto and Pinerolo.

Caprilli's *il sistema*, later known as the 'forward seat', rejected the forceful curb bit and the imposed rigidity of collection prevailing in the European cavalry schools of the day in favour of the snaffle and a system of minimal intervention. Although the cavalry schools based their teaching on classical riding, by the nineteenth century, when the schools were under pressure to turn out large numbers of men and horses in order to maintain ever bigger mounted formations, it was a much debased classicism that was reflected in the day to day instruction of both. On the other hand, Caprilli's riders were taught to 'conform to the horse's natural movement and outline' and the horses were schooled on the ground over which cavalry might be expected to operate; ditch, hedge, timber and all.

By 1904, Caprilli's system had been officially adopted and was being introduced at cavalry schools throughout Europe and the Americas. In

Britain between the two World Wars there were a number of 'Schools of Natural Equitation' purporting in varying degrees to teach Caprilli's *sistema*. At least one, under the direction of an ex-Polish officer, was still operating in South London in the late 1960s. (Britain certainly adopted the principles of forward riding, but in deference to her hunting tradition compromised with the 'balanced seat', which was taught at the cavalry school of Weedon and the Indian Army counterpart at Saugur.)

Today, the term 'natural horsemanship' has been extended to include the demonstrations given by 'whisperers' and the like, or it is applied to 'round pens' and 'join-ups'. The distinction between it and traditional riding based, more or less, on classicism has also shifted to include formal methods of teaching and management, often perceived as belonging to the 'establishment' – however that may be defined. Indeed, it may well include the sort of methods described and recommended in this book.

The appeal, I believe, is implicit in the word 'natural', with its suggestion of greater acceptability, absolving its admirers from the idea of dominant imposition in their dealings with the horse. In fact, of course, neither round pens, 'join-ups' nor even *il sistema* is 'natural', although the latter is certainly rational. (A few years ago I watched a TV programme featuring a supposedly notable Western 'horseman'. In it a young, unmade horse was pursued at a gallop over the prairie until he was to all intents exhausted. The 'team' then descended on the poor animal, who, lacking the energy to resist, submitted to being saddled, bridled, and mounted. After which, with the rider up, he was half led, half pulled alongside the older horses. The 'horseman' was clearly very pleased with himself and proud of the result. For all I know he may have considered his methods to be 'natural'. I found the whole proceeding unedifying and light years removed from the concept of the 'rational way'.)

However we ride, train or keep horses in the twenty-first century, domestication is not *natural* to an herbivorous herd animal, motivated by instincts acquired in the wild and characterized by defence/survival mechanisms derived directly from that state. Certainly, it is hardly natural for such a creature to live, as many do, without the companionship of his own kind, much less to submit to what often amounts to solitary confinement in a stable for hours at a stretch. For the same animal to accept a human sitting on his back without reacting violently is anything but natural and is, indeed, in screaming defiance of a basic instinct of survival.

Fortunately for us, 6,000 years of domestication has developed in the horse a remarkable talent for adaptation and an acceptance (more or less) of the humans on whom he is so largely dependent. Of course, there are times when he is driven into resistance and even outright rebellion, but then that's only 'natural'.

Quite certainly, the species could not survive in the twenty-first century outside of the human relationship, except in zoos, wildlife parks and those areas of the world still able to support wild horse herds. But there is a price to pay for the well-filled stomach, the warm bed and the ministrations of dedicated females (the modern equivalent, perhaps, of the priestesses of the Greek goddess, Demeter, whose image was a black mare's head).

Thus horses need to conform, within reason, to the requirements of modern society in respect of the recreational role for which the majority are kept if they are to lead settled, balanced lives. In short, there has to be an *acceptance* of the domestic state.

The mavericks, their inability to conform probably caused by unintelligent, unsympathetic handling, may in consequence be condemned to a life in which they change hands frequently as they are sent from sale to sale. If they are lucky they may come up against an owner who understands their problems and is able and willing to help them become useful members of the equestrian society. If not, the knacker's yard is likely to provide the final release for what one horseman called the 'fallen angels'.

Realistic Requirements

Given that the horse is physically capable of being ridden or driven, the requirements of the average owner are bound up in those assurances that are so frequently given in the 'Horses for Sale' columns of the equestrian journals, viz; 'Good to box, shoe, clip, etc. and quiet in traffic'.

More comprehensively, it is very desirable that the modern horse should:

1. Accept the confines of a stable and behave acceptably within it.

2. Submit to being tied without resistance and to being handled in and out of the stable.

3. Allow himself to be shod without protest.

4. Be safe and reliable in traffic within normal parameters.

5. Enter and leave trailers and horseboxes and travel quietly.

6. Behave acceptably when being clipped – certainly a requirement in most instances.

One could add that it is helpful if he can be caught up without difficulty. (Chasing recalcitrant horses is a time-wasting frustration only equalled by coping with a child who refuses to go to bed.)

It is possible for all these requirements to be met during a progressive system of training, given that the trainer is prepared to pursue the task with common sense and due application.

Finally, of course, the modern horse needs to be possessed of a high degree of *rideability*. He may be the most charming character in the stable, pick his feet up on request when being shod and stand like a rock to be clipped, but all that is to no avail without rideability, and that is the major objective throughout his education. This quality has already been defined in the introduction to this book as that of the versatile horse who is a pleasure to ride in all circumstances as a result of rational management.

Nursery and Primary School

Following his early, but crucial, 'nursery education' as a foal, the first part of the young horse's schooling begins in April of his third year, when he is introduced to the stable and the new environment of the yard and the schooling area. Taking advantage of the better weather and the longer days it continues into the following August, after which, under supervision and in receipt of a carefully formulated subsidiary diet, he is allowed to grow on naturally until he is brought up again as a four-year-old in the following April to begin his secondary education.

That may extend over the winter into the early part of the next year, when he will be five years old. After a break on the spring grass the horse, theoretically, is ready to enter into 'further education' in whichever specialist discipline seems appropriate to his talents. By no means all horses have the capability to go into specialist training and the majority of owners are, indeed, content to accept their generally nicely mannered horse as he is, while still trying to improve on their joint performance.

Foal Days

Before we become involved in the horse's primary school (where we work towards backing him), the well-brought-up youngster will have been to nursery school. On the basis of the child being father to the man a lot depends on how well and how intelligently the foal is handled virtually from the time of his birth. Certainly, within ten days or so of his entry into

'The child is father to the man.' Much of the subsequent training depends on how well, and how intelligently, the young foal is handled.

this world he will become familiar with human contact and will begin to accept it as a part of his life.

Quite soon he will be introduced to a foal slip (headcollar), put on tactfully from back to front in accordance with the precepts of classical riding. The made horse is ridden *from* the leg *into* the hand, from the back to the front, and never the other way round. The foal is haltered on the same principle, an enveloping arm round his rear pushing him gently forward *into* the open foal slip that is awaiting at the other end. It is surprising how much damage – and permanent damage, too – can be done if haltering becomes a macho exercise with two 'heavies' cornering the terrified young animal and forcing the collar onto his head. To my certain knowledge it still occurs; and not only on the Mongolian steppes.

Once the slip is accepted it does not take long to teach the rudiments of being led in-hand, *and from both sides*, accomplished again from back to front, that is, with the support of the persuasive arm round his rump.

If the handler seeks to drag the foal forward, the little animal will react as he is certain to do throughout his life, by pulling back with an equal or greater force. This procedure is about as sensible as pulling backwards on the reins when asking the horse to go forwards, and is no more productive.

Throughout this nursery education, the foal is supported by the example set by his dam and learns from it. A friendly, sensible mare passes on her own good qualities and her trust in humans to her offspring. If she accepts the stable environment calmly when she and the foal are brought in briefly for whatever purpose, the foal will follow suit. Indeed, the stable, the equivalent of the 'whisperer's' round pen, is a very good classroom.

Similarly, if the mare enters a horsebox or trailer quietly, the foal will follow rather than be separated from her. (The gravitational pull of the mare is also valuable in teaching the foal to lead. Place the mare a short distance away and the foal will surely go forward to reach her.) During this nursery period, foals will also be gradually introduced to supplementary feeding to encourage their growth.

If the foal is home-bred, the transition to primary schooling is an easy extension of what he has already learned. If the youngster is bought as a two- or three-year-old the same should apply when the purchase is made from a well-conducted stud, but there is the disadvantage of not knowing exactly what has been taught and how.

In either case, it is advisable to take nothing for granted when beginning to work with the three-year-old and to start all over again with handling, leading and so on.

The Three-Year-Old

At three, the well-fed youngster should be well-grown but *not* carrying surplus flesh. Well-grown is not the same as fully grown and the horse is still very much a baby.

This immaturity has a number of physical manifestations, which have to be taken into account if early setbacks are to be avoided. One example of

A typical three-year-old. He is well-proportioned but soft and immature.

this is the physical state of the epiphyses or 'growth plates' on the long bones of the legs, which have to be closed to allow the limbs to sustain the effects of work and, in the course of time, to work under the weight of a rider. Closure of the epiphysis at the end of the cannon bone, above the fetlock joint, is usually completed at between nine and twelve months; that at the end of the radius, immediately above the knee joint, will be closed at between two and two-and-a-half years in normal circumstances.

Inflammation of the plates causes the disease known as 'round joints' (epiphysitis). Swelling occurs and the area may become hot and tender. Epiphysitis in foals is usually found in the fetlocks: in yearlings and even in two-year-olds it occurs in the knee and hock joints. The disease is always accompanied by more or less severe lameness.

Epiphysitis can certainly be caused by premature work, but may also arise from a dietary imbalance. Usually this is caused because the phosphorus element in the important phosphorus/calcium ratio is much in excess of the calcium content, or because of a deficiency in Vitamin D (the sunlight vitamin). The phosphorus/calcium imbalance may be the result of feeding too much bran in the ration (not as likely today as it once might have been) or by giving a high-protein feed without a corresponding increase being

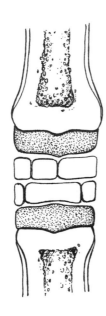

Figure 1. A diagram of the epiphyses or 'growth plates' on the long bones of the leg. Closure above the fetlock joint is completed at nine to twelve months. Closure above the knee joint will occur between two and two-and-a-half years approximately. Epiphysitis (round joints) is marked by inflammation, swelling and lameness and may be caused by premature work or, less usually, by a dietary imbalance.

made in the calcium intake. The sort of animal most prone to the condition is the youngster in 'show condition' who is allowed to become over-topped and is simply too heavy for his immature legs. Animals of this sort rarely appear later on in ridden classes and they are an unsuitable choice for schooling on as three-year-olds.

Surprisingly, little attention is given to epiphysitis, although it is more prevalent than might be imagined, particularly when the disease is mild in its form.

The three-year-old still has some growing to do and when brought up will certainly be higher behind (at the croup) than at the withers. Inevitably, on this account alone, he carries his weight over the forehand. In addition to specifics such as the growth plates, the general bone structure has yet to mature and it takes longer in some types and breeds than others. Furthermore, he is still a couple of years away from having a 'full mouth', i.e. a complete set of permanent teeth.

Similarly, the musculature is soft and undeveloped and the movement is likely to be a bit gangly and even a little uncoordinated, particularly when working on a circle.

In the same way, the young mind is no more mature than the body. Its ability to concentrate is limited and it is easily confused. Understandably, in these circumstances, behaviour, like that of the human child, can be erratic and unpredictable.

The Four-Year-Old

There is a noticeable difference in the physical appearance of the four-year-old in comparison to that of the three-year-old when first brought into work. At four, the school work, combined with the cumulative effect of good feeding from foalhood, will have resulted in a big, well-grown, strong young horse, physically and mentally ready for a more demanding work programme.

Nonetheless, the preparation needs to be gradual if the risk of sprains and strains, as well as misunderstandings, is to be avoided.

Indeed, of the two phases this is the more difficult and the more likely to throw up the odd problem. The three-year-old, like the small boy in his first term at school, is too much in awe of his teachers and his surroundings to

A very well-made four-year-old, physically able to cope with the demands of secondary training.

make any serious show of independence. Once he has submitted to the routine, he is happy enough to be co-operative while he learns to understand what is wanted of him. Towards the end of his primary schooling the young human has felt his feet, gained in confidence and lost some of his respect for authority – sufficient, indeed, for him to assert himself a bit more. Young horses are much the same and the development is to be welcomed – the last thing that is wanted is a 'mechanical' horse with built-in buttons but without character or the ability to use his own initiative.

Thus we may expect the four-year-old to be a bit cocky and without much doubt he will test the authority of his trainer, seeing how far he can chance his arm. It would not be 'natural' if he did not occasionally resist out of cussedness, but in a rational system it does not present a problem or constitute anything more than a minor irritation, if that.

The Basis of Training

The education of the young horse in both phases depends on the observance of some common-sense factors. The basis is:

1. *Preparation* of physical structure/mental capacity for the progression of ground and ridden work.

2. Teaching the horse the *acceptance* of the rider's weight and presence on his back.

3. Work and management directed at developing the body to *carry weight* easily, in balance and without risk of physical strain or discomfort that might lead to resentment.

4. Establishment and subsequent refinement of a *three-way* system of *communication* between horse and rider. On a physical plane this involves:

   a. the rider *speaking* to the horse through the medium of the aids;

   b. the rider *listening* to the horse through the latter's physical responses;

   c. horse and rider reaching a mental *rapport*, in which *the one listens to the other*.

How much can be achieved is dependent upon:

1. The rider's appreciation of *basic anatomy* as it is related to work under saddle.

2. A sympathetic understanding of the *nature* and *characteristics* of a species in which behavioural patterns are motivated by *instinct* and not by the ability to *reason*.

Other than these factors, the end result is influenced by the character of the trainer, who needs to combine *sensitivity* and *intelligence* with a *positive* attitude.

In the last respect, an appropriate theme song might be Johnny Mercer's:

> *You've got to ac-cent-tchu-ate the positive,*
> *Eli-my-nate the negative,*
> *Latch on to the affirmative*
> *Don't mess with Mister In-between.*

To which might be added: And for God's sake resist the anthropomorphic.

Beyond understanding the horse, trainers have also to understand the *theory* of riding and then to have the *physical ability* to put it into practice. Without knowing the theory it is impossible to put it into practice. William Steinkraus, the American showjumping captain and Olympic gold medallist, summarized it admirably when he wrote: '… *understanding* equitation makes *doing* it correctly immeasurably easier…'

Finally, the *facilities* available have a bearing upon what can be achieved and in what space of time. They are examined in the opening section of Part 2.

Essential Anatomy

It is not necessary for the majority of riders to have an in-depth knowledge of equine physiology and structure, but without a good basic understanding one is to all intents working in the dark without knowing what one is attempting to achieve. However, armed with a good, working knowledge and bearing in mind the seemingly paradoxical principle of *back to front*, it is remarkable how easily the schooling exercises fall into place.

Back to Front

Back to front provides a fundamental guide pattern because it is a continual reminder that our efforts are directed at modifying the natural anatomy of the horse to conform more nearly to the demands made on the structure when the horse is ridden.

The fundamental requirement is the carrying of weight on the back, which, in its natural state, is not very well suited to the purpose. The equine structure is like that of a bridge, and not one built to the best engineering principles. The two supporting piers at either end are strong enough but the centre of its span is woefully weak. Instead of being shaped in the rounded arch essential to its strength, it actually dips in the middle. The result of putting weight on an immature, natural back is to cause it to hollow, locking the spinal vertebrae and so inhibiting the movement. The horse is then compelled to take on a V-shape, head and neck raised at one end like that of a camel, while the hind legs, the means of propulsion, are left to trail painfully behind. The appropriately graphic horsy term is 'hind legs in the next county'.

In pursuit of the back-to-front principle our job is to encourage, by rational exercise, the hind legs to become engaged *under* the body, thus increasing the propulsive power, causing a rounding of the top-line and a freeing of the spinal process. As we progress and the hind legs become increasingly engaged, the shoulders, neck and head are raised, the weight is carried more over the quarters and the forehand is *lightened*. Eureka!

All this is made possible by the proper development of the musculature and the use made of ligaments – particularly the powerful, elastic *ligamentum nuchae* (cervical ligament) running from the poll to behind the withers, and then, in less elastic form and under a slightly altered name, *ligamentum nucho-dorsale* (supraspinous ligament), along the top of the spinal column to the sacrum at the horse's croup.

Skeleton, Muscles, Tendons and Ligaments

But, as in all things, it is best to begin at the beginning: in this instance with the skeleton, the framework of the body that is made up of variously shaped bones. These support the body mass and it is their movement, activated by joints, in conjunction with muscles, that produces movement in the whole body.

A joint is formed at the junction of two bones and while representing an engineering feat of some magnitude, it is, at least potentially, the weakest part of the structure. The ends of the bones making a joint, the articular surfaces, are of greater density than will be found elsewhere in the bone so

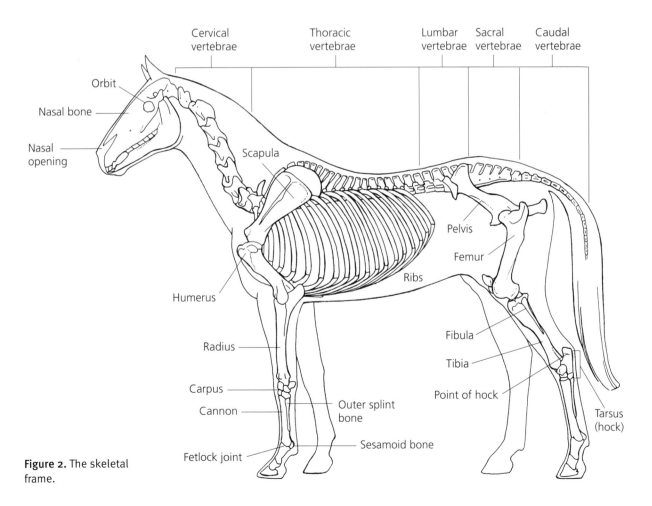

Figure 2. The skeletal frame.

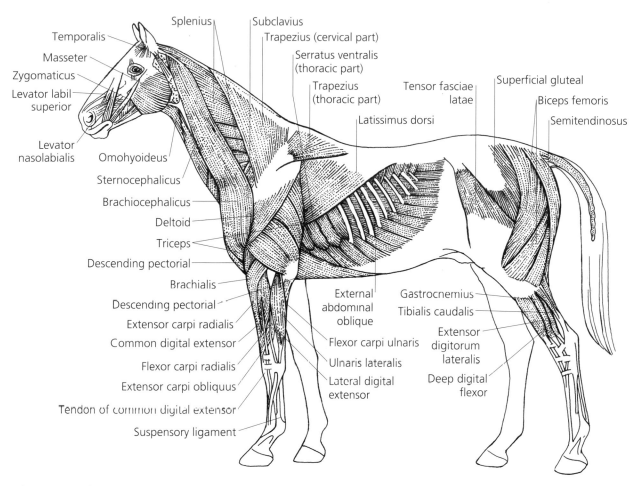

Temporalis
Masseter
Zygomaticus
Levator labil superior
Levator nasolabialis
Omohyoideus
Sternocephalicus
Brachiocephalicus
Deltoid
Triceps
Descending pectorial
Brachialis
Descending pectorial
Extensor carpi radialis
Common digital extensor
Flexor carpi radialis
Extensor carpi obliquus
Tendon of common digital extensor
Suspensory ligament

Splenius
Subclavius
Trapezius (cervical part)
Serratus ventralis (thoracic part)
Trapezius (thoracic part)
Latissimus dorsi
Tensor fasciae latae
Superficial gluteal
Biceps femoris
Semitendinosus

External abdominal oblique
Flexor carpi ulnaris
Ulnaris lateralis
Lateral digital extensor

Gastrocnemius
Tibialis caudalis
Extensor digitorum lateralis
Deep digital flexor

Figure 3. Muscle structure.

Figure 4. A joint is formed at the junction of two bones and is probably the weakest part of the structure. Damage to the joint is most likely to cause lameness.

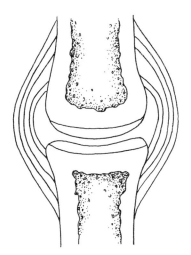

as to be better able to withstand the friction that occurs between the surfaces. But that, in itself, would not prevent unacceptable wear and so the surfaces are separated by a layer of gristle, called cartilage. The whole joint is held together by ligaments, tough, fibrous and flexible tissues which are attached to each bone. These also serve the essential purpose of limiting the joint's movement so that it cannot be extended beyond its capability.

To complete this remarkable structure and give added protection against damage, the joint is encased within a two-layer capsule. The outer layer, holding the joint firmly, gives added support while the inner secretes an oily fluid (synovia, or joint oil), allowing the joint to work within a vessel of oil and therefore in a state of constant lubrication.

Any damage to a ligament is serious. It can cause lameness and, clearly, will affect the efficiency of the joint to which it is connected. Similarly, damage to a joint (as a result of a blow, for instance), that causes inflammation and swelling, affects its working capacity and may well be accompanied by lameness. The same is true of any disease occurring in the joint.

Muscle covers a large part of the body and is attached to bones to produce movement in the joints and thus in the body mass. Skeletal muscles act in pairs, one of which contracts while the other extends. Active movement is produced by the contracting muscle drawing together two points of attachment to initiate the action of the joint. However, that cannot be done by muscle alone, since muscle, though possessed of elasticity, would be easily torn or strained. To obviate that sort of damage, it is equipped with tendons, the tough, inelastic ropes connecting muscle with bone. To all intents, tendon is plaited into the substance of the muscle at one end while being attached firmly to the actual bone at the other, activating the joint in response to the contraction or extension of the connected muscle.

Just as damage to a ligament affects the movement, so any damage to the tendon will also impair the action more or less seriously, depending upon the extent of the damage sustained.

Particular strain is placed on the tendons by galloping over broken or uneven terrain, even if it is no more than gently undulating. When this is combined with jumping obstacles or negotiating natural hazards, the danger is increased correspondingly. For this reason it is advisable when riding competitively cross-country to give protection and support to the lower legs by means of well-constructed boots or carefully fitted bandages.

Poor shoeing, or neglected feet ('those shoes will do for another week yet') that result in the foot growing too long and the heel being too low on the ground, both contribute to tendon problems in the lower leg.

Condition and Co-ordination

Both these factors are major sources of tendon damage. Obviously, horses who are galloped and jumped when in unfit condition will be more susceptible to injury, especially when the ground is rough and uneven. Unfit horses – and very tired ones also – lack that degree of tension in the muscles which is called *tonus* or *muscle tone*. It is this slight but necessary state of tension that prevents the convulsive or spasmodic sort of movement which could cause joints to flex or extend so violently as to be damaged.

Lack of muscle tone and subsequently co-ordination of the limbs is noticeable and not unnatural in young horses at the outset of their training. On the whole, they manage pretty well at liberty, but the risk of injury is increased by confinement and artificial feeding which leads to their letting off steam when they are released to the freedom of the paddock. It is good to see young horses at liberty expressing their *joie de vivre* by galloping, bucking, jumping and generally turning themselves inside out, but that is when they are most vulnerable to strains, sprains and accidental knocks. However, beyond taking common-sense precautions and monitoring the food intake carefully, there is really not much else that can be done.

Protection

More can be done to safeguard the young horse during the early lessons. A good set of protective and supportive boots all round is an obvious precaution, but just as important is to limit the time of the schooling periods. Initially they need to be kept short – twenty minutes is quite long enough – and they should only be increased by gradual stages, and then by not a lot.

If the horse is overworked and becomes tired he loses his muscle tone and work becomes a penance rather than a pleasure. Injury is then more likely, while we also risk the possibility of his being made resentful and rebellious.

Indeed, throughout the training it is unwise to overwork. (I have a neighbour, a dedicated and determined horsewoman, who has yet to learn to concede graciously when her horse is telling her plainly that enough is enough. Instead she will persevere with a movement until the horse is not only tired but confused also. Fortunately, as is often the case, the horse has the last word. On more than one occasion he has bided his time and then dumped her in salutary fashion, and very painfully, over the school rails. Alas, by then the damage is done and the relationship irretrievably lost.)

The best maxim is to hasten slowly. For those who still prefer the faster route I would advise doing fifty press-ups without pause. Those unused to this form of masochism will find the point made clearly and very quickly.

Muscle Function

A peculiar property of muscle, relevant to schooling, is its ability to contract and to be extended. In fact, muscle will stretch to the same extent that it can be contracted and vice versa. It follows, therefore, that the greater the ability of muscle to extend and contract, the nearer the joints will be to flexing to the limits of their capacity in promoting optimum movement.

We are then bound to conclude that to obtain maximum contraction we must first encourage extension of the muscles.

With regard to the stretching process, an important group of muscles are those running from the neck on either side of the spine to form the top-line of the horse. They are arranged in pairs on either side of the *ligamentum nuchae*, the cervical ligament. By inducing the horse to stretch and lower the head and neck, this ligament and its accompanying muscle structure are stretched; a matter facilitated by the ligament passing over the fulcrum provided by the withers. The spine of the horse then achieves a necessary degree of tension and the back itself becomes arched and rounded as, indeed, the hind legs become more actively engaged.

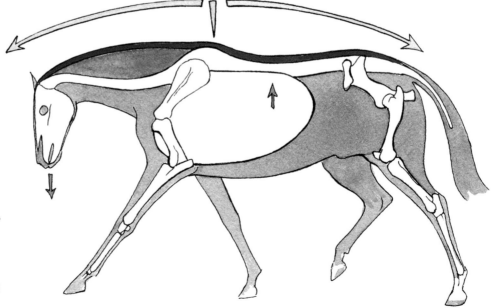

Figure 5. The engagement of the hind legs accompanies the rounding of the top-line, brought about by the stretching of the powerful cervical ligament (coloured red) over the fulcrum formed by the withers.

The muscles with which we are concerned are the voluntary muscles and they are of two kinds: flexors, those that contract to flex the joint, and extensors, the ones that do the opposite.

The muscles are, therefore, acting in pairs, but they can also act to either *oppose* or *compensate*. In the rounding of the top-line, for example, the big back muscles, acting as *extensors*, are stretched, the rounding effect being completed by the increased engagement of the hind legs accompanied by the raising of the abdomen. Three muscles on the sides of the abdomen and three running from the fifth and ninth ribs to the pubis act as *flexors* in opposition to the extending muscles of the back.

The head and neck are supported in the same way so that they are carried without conscious effort; the muscles on the underside of the neck, in the chest region, being matched by the opposing tension of the muscles lying on the top of the neck.

Lack of development in any of the muscles or an inability to extend and contract sufficiently make it more difficult, even impossible, to obtain the desired riding outline together with the carriage and the subsequent action that constitute mechanical efficiency.

The carriage of head and neck, if imposed by the hands and/or artificial means, results in the hollowed, U-shaped outline already described. Conversely, it should be obtained by development of the muscles of the whole of the top-line, through a rational schooling technique.

To an extent, however, it will also depend upon the initial skeletal conformation and there is little to be done about that except to avoid the worst sort of conformational deficiencies. If, for example, one is unfortunate enough to have a horse with a large, heavy head carried on a long, weak neck (the worst possible conformation) there is an in-built problem on account of the former being too heavy for the latter to support. The neck can, certainly, be strengthened by intelligent schooling (ground-poles causing the horse to stretch and lower go some way to help) but the defect is fundamental and is not going to be eradicated entirely.

In addition to the compensatory action that helps to establish longitudinal carriage, another example of compensatory muscle action is when the horse 'bends' on a circle or the elements of one. In this instance the muscles involved are the dorsal muscles on either side of the spine and the lateral flexors of the trunk.

In fact, the horse does not 'bend', if by that it is meant that his spine is curved to correspond with the arc of the movement. That is impossible, because the spine, other than in the neck and tail regions, is a relatively rigid

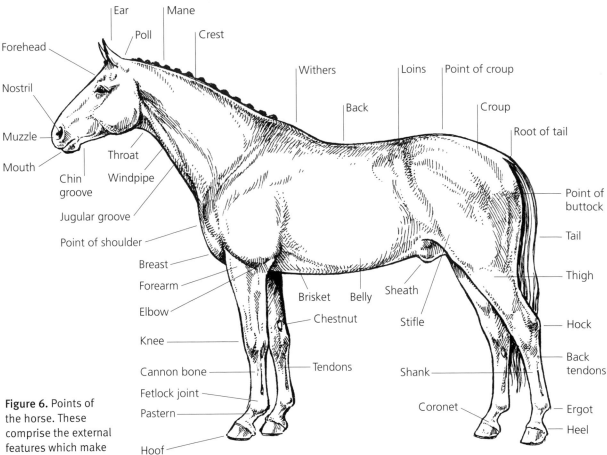

Figure 6. Points of the horse. These comprise the external features which make up the animal's conformation.

structure in the lateral plane, capable of a lateral deviation of a few inches at the most. This being so, you cannot 'bend' the horse round your inside leg, although you can go through the motions.

What happens is that, in making a turn or following the arc of a circle, the muscles on the inside of the body *contract* to correspond with the arc, while those on the outside allow for the contraction by being extended. We then have the *appearance* of the horse being bent round the inside leg but not in reality.

What is absolutely certain is that unless there is equal development of the muscles on both sides of the body (a situation rarely achieved in its entirety) the horse will favour one side or the other and will not bend in both directions with equal facility. In extreme instances the animal will then become labelled as 'one-sided' and the less experienced, as well sometimes as the very experienced, will have recourse to peculiarly shaped bits and restrictive reins of ingenious design, rather than employing a rational system of schooling and riding to eliminate the difficulty. The latter does not take any longer and it is the only certain way to balance one side against the other.

Finally, since there are voluntary muscles there have also to be *involuntary* ones. These are those working on the internal organs, like those causing bowel movement, and the *cardiac* muscle connected with that function.

The Nervous System

Muscles certainly produce movement by activating joints but it is the nervous system that is central to the process.

In simple terms, muscles and organs send signals to the spinal cord via a nerve. That either triggers an unconscious response or the signal is relayed to the brain and dealt with consciously.

Nerves fall into two categories. There are the *sensory* nerves, which allow the animal to feel, see, hear, smell and taste without conscious effort, and the *motor* nerves which are those concerned with motion. It is thought that, within limits, the contraction of which the muscle is capable is proportionate to the degree of stimulation provided by its nerves.

It follows that the strength and sensitivity of the nervous system will govern the speed of the reflexes, and that is very relevant to both the selection and training of horses. In the most general terms the reactions of the common-bred, cold-blood horses, like, to take an extreme example, the ugly duckling of the heavy breeds, the French Poitevin or Mulassier, are far slower than those of the well-bred riding horse having a percentage of Arabian or Thoroughbred blood. The Poitevin breeds the best mules in Europe but its nervous system, while adequate for the purpose, is not a very efficient one, while that of the quick-moving, highly tuned Thoroughbred can, of course, be embarrassingly efficient. One could sit on a Poitevin and give him an almighty kick in the ribs that might just cause the skin on the flanks to twitch a little, but do that to a Thoroughbred and he would explode.

(The Poitevin, as well as providing the base stock for a mule breeding industry, also drained the marshes of La Vendee and Poitou in the seventeenth century. That was brutally hard work, which the Poitevin tackled reliably, effectively and without making a fuss. Thoroughbreds don't breed mules and they would be hopeless at draining marshes. Even so, I do not advise the purchase of a Poitevin as a riding horse.)

Balance and Conformation

Balance is as much a preoccupation to the horseman as the weather is to the British public.

If the horse were just a rectangular body mass supported on four pillars, the body would be balanced in the centre of the rectangle. In the same way, the point of balance on a child's see-saw is the central support that forms a pivot for the movement. But, of course, the horse is not simply a rectangle, because there is the addition of a head and neck at one end. One end is therefore heavier than the other and in consequence, as Figures 7 and 8 show, the point of balance is moved forward of the centre.

Erudite academics, veterinarians and hippologists have conducted experiments to establish beyond reasonable doubt that the centre of balance of the horse standing square at rest, with the head and neck carried naturally, and with the weight distributed equally over all four feet, is at the intersection of an imaginary line passing vertically from a point a little to the rear of the withers, *through the centre of his body* to the ground, and a second line drawn horizontally, through the centre of the body, between the point of the shoulder to the buttock. That is generally accepted, certainly so far as the horse of proportionate conformation is concerned.

However, a less than perfect conformation can alter the position of the centre. If, for example, there is a thick, heavy neck supporting a similarly heavy head, more weight will be carried over the forehand and the point of balance

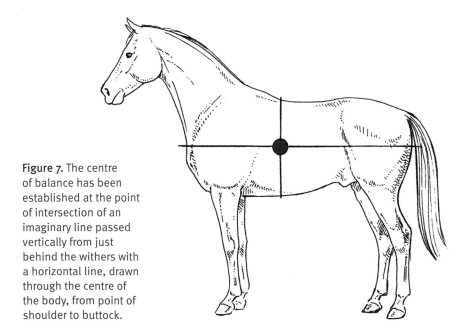

Figure 7. The centre of balance has been established at the point of intersection of an imaginary line passed vertically from just behind the withers with a horizontal line, drawn through the centre of the body, from point of shoulder to buttock.

shifts forward commensurately. Conversely, a tiny head on a short, thin neck will cause the point to be positioned to the rear of the accepted position.

Nor is the point of balance static, a matter that should be clearly appreciated by riders. When the horse is moving at speed, with head and neck

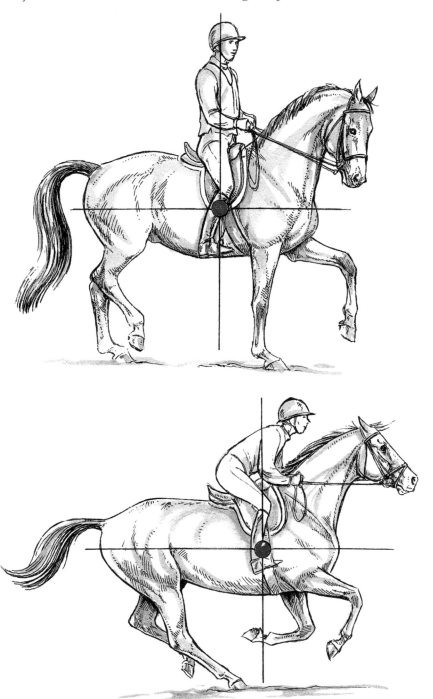

Figure 8. The rider in balance, the weight carried over the centre of the horse's balance.

extended, or at the moment of take-off at a fence, the point moves forward. In the state of collection, when the neck is held high and the face is positioned almost in the vertical plane, the horse's base is shortened by the hind legs being strongly engaged under the body and the quarters are lowered in consequence. Then, the point of balance shifts at least a little towards the rear. Similarly, when the horse turns or moves laterally, the centre of balance is shifted to the side in the direction of the movement.

In effect, head and neck, corresponding to a sort of pendulum, are being used as a balancing agent for the body mass. Galloping over broken ground, for instance, the horse maintains equilibrium by raising or lowering the balancing agent according to the terrain.

It follows that, for the rider to be in balance, the rider's weight must be carried as nearly as possible over the horse's centre of balance. Carried too far forward it will overweight the forehand, carried too far to the rear it inhibits the engagement of the hind legs and the propulsive thrust.

Assessing conformation is all about correct symmetrical proportions suitable for the purpose intended, in this context the riding horse. The proportionate horse is also a mechanically efficient one and will be less prone to unsoundness and strain and, all else being equal, may be expected to enjoy a longer active life. Since the well-proportioned horse will be naturally balanced, the movement will be free and economical and there will be a potentially higher performance level.

On the other hand, deficiencies in conformation impose limitations on the horse. In extreme circumstances, an animal forced by whatever means into an outline that causes him discomfort because of proportional failings in his structure, is very likely to become resentful and to resist in whatever way is open to him.

Figure 9, illustrating Professor Wortley-Axe's system of measurement for the ideally proportioned light horse, is instructive and represents the most authoritative guide to conformation available to us, although it may not correspond exactly to the proportions of the still immature three-year-old. (Wortley-Axe was a President of the Royal College of Veterinary Surgeons, a prolific writer and author of the ten-volume work, *The Horse*, published in 1905.)

Wortley-Axe's system of assessment is based on two principal units; the length of the head, and the distance between point of buttock and hip. The system is founded on the studies of a handful of expert French veterinarians, beginning with Claude Bourgelat (1712–1779), the first principal of the Royal Veterinary School of Lyons, which was established in 1762, almost

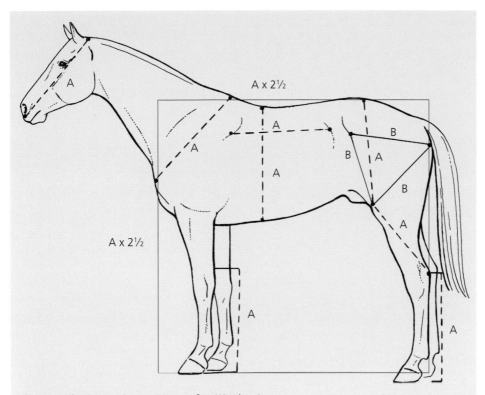

Figure 9. The Proportionate Horse after Wortley-Axe.
Proportions are based on two principal units of measurement:
1. length of head (A); 2. distance between seat-bone (point of buttock) and point of hip (B).
Length of head (A) = (a) point of hock to ground; (b) point of hock to fold of stifle;
(c) chestnut to base of foot; (d) depth of body at girth; (e) posterior angle of scapula
(shoulder-blade), at rear of its junction with the withers, to the point of hip;
(f) fold of stifle to croup; (g) withers to point of shoulder.
Seat-bone–point of hip (B) = (a) seat-bone to stifle; (b) stifle to point of hip (c) point of hip
to seat-bone.
Length from point of shoulder to seat-bone = length of head x 2½.
Height from fetlock to elbow = height from elbow to withers.
Length of neck (relatively long for speed) = approx. 1½ times measurement from poll,
down front of face, to lower lip.

thirty years before the foundation of the school in London which was to become the Royal Veterinary College. The French experts, notably Professors Duhousset, Goubaux and Barrier, worked on comparative measurements and observations made between hundreds and, if necessary, thousands of horses with the object of relating conformation to specific purposes.

Of course, there never was a perfect horse and never will be, so do not be too concerned if your ewe-lamb fails to measure up to the Professor's ideal. Indeed, one may take heart from the observation made by Goubaux and Barrier. These gentlemen, with much meticulous research into the manner in

Figure 10.
Conformational defects affecting action.

(a) Front view, left to right: correct; base wide; base narrow; knock knees; pigeon toes.

(b) Rear view, left to right: correct; base wide; base narrow; cow hocks; bow legs.

which defects in conformation are compensated, produced a voluminous paper entitled *Compensation of Defect of Conformation*, concluding that: 'It frequently happens that a good quality annuls a defect, or that one defect may be counterbalanced by another whose influence is diametrically opposite.'

Nonetheless, notable conformational faults will without doubt create schooling problems in relation to balance and they disturb, more or less seriously, the centre of gravity. (The point of balance, discussed previously, was, in fact, determined by research made by Professor Colin of London and was confirmed by Goubaux and Barrier in Paris.)

The conformation best-suited to speed in the horse, and, to a degree, to athleticism is associated with *length* in the overall proportions, in the limbs

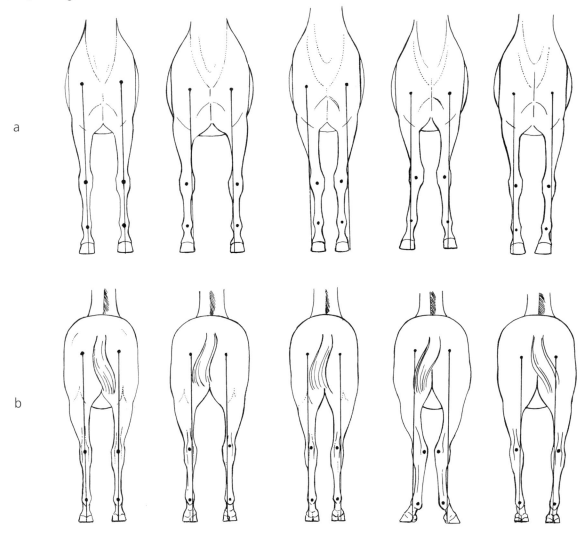

a

b

Figure 11. Faulty action. *Top left* – base narrow, going close behind; *top right* – pigeon toes, plaiting; *bottom left* – base narrow, going close in front; *bottom right* – dishing or, euphemistically, 'round-actioned'.

and the musculature. *Short* proportions, heavy bones and short, thick muscles are, on the other hand, indicative of the structure's strength and tractive power. Although he may be lacking in speed and scope, the short, stuffy type of horse will sometimes have considerable gymnastic ability.

Size

Is size important? Clearly, it is if you are 1.52 m (5 ft) tall and are confronted with a 17.2 hh gargantuan or, conversely, if you are tall and heavily built and come up against a blood-weed of no more than 15 hh. Interestingly, Wortley-Axe and his colleagues, working at a time when the world's economy was dependent on horse-power, could suggest 15.3 hh as being the ideal. After an extensive study of height in relation to proportion, pace and overall efficiency they put forward 15.3 hh as being the 'limit of stature' for a riding horse 'within which the greatest usefulness is to be found'.

It is true that big horses, at 17 hh and over, are rarely as gymnastically adept as the smaller ones and are, on purely mechanical grounds, probably less efficient; while it is also thought that they are more prone to respiratory problems. If they have an advantage it is that they make the fences look smaller.

Sex

Is sex important? Well, it makes the world go round and there is some significance when it comes to the choice of a horse – if, indeed, that choice enters the equation.

Stallions are not an option for the majority of one- or two-horse owners; geldings are usually less demanding and are easier to train, while some mares can be touchy and temperamental when in season. But a good mare is frequently bold and generous and, of course, there is the possibility of breeding from her at one time or another.

I have ridden stallions, but never owned one, and confess that I found them exciting, responsive and wonderfully high-couraged. Most of my horses have been geldings and there have been some very, very good ones but I do have a soft spot for the mares. They are, after all, complete horses in the way that stallions are described as being 'entire'. I find them more challenging – I won't say more intelligent – but they are responsive, gener-ous and usually more sensitive than geldings. Very occasionally, one may correct a boisterous young gelding with a slap across his rump. It would, for me, be unthinkable to treat a mare in that way. It is more appropriate to enter into negotiations to resolve the misunderstanding.

However, a 'funny' mare can be very 'funny' and stretch one's tolerance up to and even beyond the limit. Infuriatingly, these are often the most tal-ented once you get on the right side of them. (Despite my mother's advice to avoid entanglement with red-haired ladies, I once bought a bright chest-nut mare who lived up to all the things said about chestnut mares.)

Nature and Characteristics

While an appreciation of anatomy and movement is fundamental in the context of training and riding, an understanding of the horse's nature and of the characteristics and instincts that make up the horse's personality is equally essential.

Evolution of the Horse

Equus caballus, the modern horse, derives from the small, multi-toed mammal that had evolved some 65 million years ago in the Eocene Period of the Cenozoic era. Abandoning the formal nomenclature (*hyracotherium*), American scientists called the animal Eohippus, the Dawn Horse, and it is from this browsing mammal, no larger than a middle-size dog, that the modern horse can be traced.

Eohippus gives us no insight into the personality of the horse, other than being herbivorous. He lived in a forest environment with soft ground underfoot and where the edges of water-holes would have been marshy – hence the toes and the accompanying pad, like that on a dog's paw. The pad is the only feature of Eohippus to persist in *Equus caballus* and can be seen as a small, horny callosity on the point of the fetlock that serves no purpose at all. Today, we call it the 'ergot'.

Nonetheless, Eohippus, like his descendants, epitomized the over-whelming power of environment in the process of evolution that ensures the survival only of those best fitted to adapt to their surroundings.

The animal's eyes were set centrally on the head, for there was no need of the lateral vision so necessary to his descendants.

The teeth were short-crowned, like those of pigs or monkeys, and ideally suited to the consumption of the soft leaves to be found on low-growing shrubs. But the environment for small, non-aggressive, herbivorous mammals was a hostile one in which Eohippus was preyed upon by the larger carnivores, among them the giant, flightless birds like the flesh-eating *Diatryma*.

The defensive system developed by Eohippus in consequence was based on concealment rather than otherwise, the animal having a blotched or even striped coat that provided an effective camouflage in a forest background.

From this unlikely beginning, the road leading to *Equus caballus* went onwards by fits and starts over a period of millions of years. The benchmark in the equine progression was made in the Miocene period (25–10 million years ago) when it accelerated and changed course dramatically. The extreme climatic changes that occurred during this period had a radical effect on the existing environment. Swamp and jungle land disappeared to give way to treeless plains and savannah supporting the growth of hitherto rare grasses (the *Gramineae*). These provided a plentiful, nutritious source of food for those strains of animals that were able to adapt to the altered circumstances, while those unable to do so, like the mammoth Megahippus, became extinct.

Over vast periods of time the new habitat enforced the metamorphosis of Eohippus from a browsing animal, whose principal defence was in concealment, to a grazer with highly developed defence mechanisms based on flight. These characteristics are at the core of the equine personality and remain so today despite the passage of successive millennia and the effects of domestication.

Physically, the limbs grew longer to give greater speed, and about 6 million years ago the transformation was in its final stages when the toes merged into a single hoof.

The neck, too, became longer, to allow feeding at ground level, and the dentition altered to cope with the ingestion of abrasive grasses, the newly developed molar teeth being used in a grinding action.

The eyes were placed more to the side of the head to give what amounted to all-round vision, even when their owner was head down and engaged in the act of grazing at hoof level.

These physical changes were accompanied by a commensurate heightening of the senses and reflexes, possibly stimulated to a degree by the higher protein diet afforded by a plentiful variety of nutritious grasses. (In the same way modern horses become noticeably quicker in their nervous reactions when fed at a high protein/energy level.)

Instinctive Behaviour and Characteristics

Herd behaviour in the wild

Of paramount importance is the influence of the herd, offering its members protection and security. It is this gregarious herd instinct, giving rise to sensitive defensive mechanisms, that is integral to the horse's personality and governs much of the animal's behavioural pattern. The 'gravitational pull' of the herd in its domestic form can cause minor difficulties in training, although not of any great significance. Conversely, it can be used to our advantage in a number of ways.

It is a common misconception to attribute leadership of the herd to a single dominant stallion. In reality, a wild herd is composed of a number of family groups in which a pecking order is quickly established in much the same way as in a group of domestic horses. More often than not the group is controlled by a strong-minded old matriarch, more than able to cope with the boisterous behaviour of unruly young colts. In those parts of the world

sustaining large, semi-feral herds, like those found on the Eurasian steppes, the Argentine and parts of eastern Europe, for example, the herd leader is an old, steady 'bell mare' who wears a bell collar round her neck to indicate her whereabouts. It would, indeed, be a mistake to regard mares as being generally submissive. They are just as likely to be dominant characters as stallions or, for that matter, as their human counterparts.

The role of the stallion in the wild, or in those semi-feral herds in which a stallion is run out with mares and young stock, is, nonetheless, predominant and never more so than in the mating season. At those times the natural urge to reproduce becomes paramount and sexually motivated behaviour more evident.

Otherwise, the prime motivation of the wild herd was the search for food, the horses moving slowly from one grazing ground to the next. By experience and from the example of their elders, young horses learned to avoid boggy ground in which they might become entrapped or which might increase their vulnerability to attack.

Usually, too, wild herds avoided crossing water, probably because river beds might offer a less than firm foothold; nor would they cross a swiftly running river that might sweep the young ones off their feet and carry them downstream. Modern-day horses still display apprehension when asked to enter water, and when they jump into water, as they do on cross-country

The herd instinct governs much of the animal's behavioural pattern and offers protection and security.

35

courses, a deeply rooted instinct has become subsidiary to training within the domestic context.

Always present in the wild herds was the awareness of attack by predatory carnivores like mountain lions or wolf packs. To this day, the British Exmoor ponies, one of the oldest breeds in the world, are noticeably nervous of dogs, possibly because they give rise to atavistic memories of attacks by wolf packs. The Exmoors run in semi-feral herds on their moorland habitat and on the approach of dogs, or even a group of riders, they have been observed to react by taking up a defensive 'wolf alert' formation. A tight circle is formed with the foals at its centre. The adults face inwards to present a wall of hind feet ready to repulse an attack, and then the formation turns slowly on its axis like a well-drilled rugby scrum. Meanwhile, the stallion faces the danger from outside the circle and with his rear covered by the formation is ready to see off an attacker with teeth and slashing forefeet.

The ultimate predator then as now was man, himself, but he only entered the scenario some 14 million years ago, and then as a small creature labelled by researchers *Ramapithecus* (Rama's ape). *Australopithecus* 'Ape-man', his descendant, was however hunting 6 million years ago in the time of *Pliohippus*, the first single-hooved ancestor of the modern horse.

The herd is instinctively protective of its young.

In the wild herds the first intimation of impending danger from whatever source, whether real or imagined, activated the panic button, putting the herd into immediate and unreasoning flight. If a predator was close enough to attempt to bring down the quarry by jumping on his back, the horse reacted with violent leaps and bucks in an attempt to dislodge the attacker.

Today, when a horse bucks it may be no more than an expression of *joie-de-vivre* and can be regarded as such. Bucking with intent to dislodge the rider is rather different. It can be an explosion of sheer bad temper, but it can also be the final resistance expressing discomfort and extreme frustration. When the buck is made out of alarm at some unexpected occurrence it is not unreasonable in that circumstance to see it as a momentary return to the wild condition.

Young horses, will, of course, let off steam by bucking and galloping at play –'horseplay', in fact. However, when the wild herd galloped it did so in a state of collective panic that had been provoked by some threatened danger. Otherwise, galloping for fun was a pointless exercise, expending energy unnecessarily and interfering with the serious business of feeding.

'Horseplay' – like children in the playground, young horses need to let off steam.

The domestic 'herd'

In domestication the 'herd' may be as small as two or three animals sharing a fenced paddock of a few acres and being dependent on the human agency for food over and above that offered by their limited grazing.

Their situation is a long way from the wild herds of pre-history but the survival instincts that are the legacy of the wild state do not disappear entirely. The horse remains as ever an herbivorous herd animal with an in-built defence system based on highly developed senses and the ability to take instant flight. Without doubt the instincts are to an extent subdued and kept within acceptable limits by association with humans, and by training that inculcates the habit of obedience and in which the horse learns to trust the rider – and vice versa.

The larger domestic herds, other than those comprising a mare band and young stock, are exemplified by police and military formations and by riding schools. Such horses, well-managed and enjoying an orderly lifestyle and a regular routine, undoubtedly gain in their feelings of security from being members of a close-knit family.

But even the cosy, happy family atmosphere can have its drawbacks. There have, for example, been a number of instances when a trooper, ordered to carry a message to another formation, has had difficulty in persuading his horse to observe army regulations and leave his companions. Similarly,

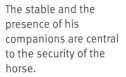

The stable and the presence of his companions are central to the security of the horse.

riding school horses, happy enough when being ridden in a group, are frequently reluctant to hack out on their own. The purchase of a school horse who has been a favourite when taking lessons is certainly a matter to be approached with due caution. All too frequently the well-behaved, obedient animal in the riding school undergoes a personality change when he becomes 'privately owned' and begins a new life as a 'single horse'.

These are probably extreme examples and on the whole the modern, intelligently schooled horse with a properly balanced outlook does not experience difficulty in rejecting the temporary herd condition to perform individually. Show-jumpers leave the collecting ring and their companions of the moment to jump a course of fences in an arena – although the wise course-builder starts his course with easier straightforward obstacles, placing the more difficult ones at the end of the track where it begins to turn back to the collecting ring and the security of the herd. Event horses most certainly perform in isolation and usually far outside the field of 'gravitational pull' centred on the stable and the collecting rings.

In teaching young horses to jump it is no more than common sense to take advantage of their natural inclination and follow the guiding precept of *make it easy for the horse*. Have the first introduction to a small fence sited towards the stable or yard so that he is jumping towards home and not vice versa. In open country, a young horse benefits from following an old-stager over an obstacle. The force of example certainly plays a part but that he follows is just as much because he does not wish to be separated from his companion.

The introductions to traffic are another example of employing the attraction of the stable to encourage the young horse's acceptance of road vehicles. It is noticeable that all horses perk up and stride out more enthusiastically as they turn for home. The thinking trainer takes advantage of this natural reaction by planning the exercise route over the quieter lanes on the way out and returning on the busier roads that carry a greater traffic flow. By then the horse's mind is becoming preoccupied with the proximity of the stable and the feed which he knows is awaiting his return. In that state of mind he is less likely to be too concerned by lorries, buses and so on.

Security

Security is just as much a basic need of the horse as it is of the human and in the domestic horse his familiar surroundings, in particular his stable, become the focal centre supplying that need. The stable is, indeed, of enormous importance in training and management but only, of course, if it is supported by the quiet, sensible attitude of the people handling the horse.

In a perfect state, the stable is always a place to be associated with pleasurable experience: comfort, shelter, relaxation, safety and, of course, *food*, a prime consideration in the horse's life. In reality, that sort of perfection is unattainable, which is no bad thing. Horses, like humans, have to accept the less than perfect experience if they are to be properly balanced individuals. We cannot avoid the visits of the vet, if not to treat injury then to administer the necessary injections which, in the well-run yard, are to all intents mandatory.

Sometimes, young horses, like young children, need to be corrected for momentary lapses of good manners. A young horse may be rough and pushy in his box; he may, in certain circumstances, take a nip at you or even raise a leg to threaten. Were he to behave like that with his own kind he could expect retaliation and it is no different in his domestic relationship with man. Not for a moment would I countenance the *punishment* of a horse either in his box or elsewhere. Indeed, most minor misdemeanours are best ignored. (The only way to treat the little boy intent on shocking us by entering the drawing room and pronouncing the ultimate rudery, 'Pot, po, bum, lavatory' is to take no notice at all. The same treatment is just as effective when horses pull faces at us as we move round the box.) However, if correction is needed, apply it firmly and immediately, but without shouting –

He finds the touch at his girth irritating and responds by 'making faces'.

if you must open your mouth let it be in a brief, low growl. It will be both sufficient and salutary.

The positive aspect in such circumstances is that if the box (like the human home) is established as the centre of the animal's security, the occasional deserved reprimand and even the ministrations of the veterinary surgeon are more easily accepted by its occupant.

Leadership

Security is certainly concerned with routine and familiarity but it is also involved with the quality of leadership. In the wild, the authority of the group leader is accepted; in domestication that role is increasingly taken by the trainer. But acceptance is by no means automatic. *Respect has to be earned.*

In an egalitarian society, *partnership* between horse and rider is an attractive philosophy. It is, after all, essential to the horse/human relationship, but we would be unwise to think of it as an equal partnership. The human has always to be the senior partner of the two, otherwise we are in danger of falling into equine-led anarchy.

Just how the senior partner retains his or her position depends a lot upon the dominant/recessive factor, of which elements occur in varying degrees in both horses and humans.

The temptation, and it is a common enough human reaction, is to

Signs of aggression are commonplace in groups comprising the herd as individuals establish a 'pecking order'.

respond to the dominant horse in his own terms, attempting to obtain submission by being even more dominant. The ensuing battle of wills is rarely, if ever, conclusive and can end with a rebellious, resentful horse and an unhappy, frustrated owner.

It is wiser to meet the horse halfway, persuading him into doing what is wanted even to the point of allowing him to think the initiative is his own. If he goes too fast, let him think that we are quite happy with that speed: if he jumps too big for comfort we will go along with that, too. It is from such a point that we can begin to contain his courage and enthusiasm within acceptable limits.

Conversely, if the rider begins to fight him it will only provoke an even more forceful response and, in trials of strength, the odds are on the hugely more powerful horse.

The recessive horse is, by contrast, unsure of himself and lacking in confidence. He is not helped by our being over-protective or even over-sympathetic.

His need is for strong, dominant leadership that never descends to rough treatment, of course, but leaves him in no doubt as to what is wanted of him. That sort of leadership gives him increasing confidence *and* a sense of security.

Timidity

We all appreciate that, despite his size and strength, the horse is really the most 'timorous beastie'. This is natural in a non-aggressive herbivore relying for his defence on instant flight, but it can be irritating. On that count we have to be careful of our reactions to apparently illogical and sometimes unseating behaviour.

A rustle in a hedgerow, a sudden noise, an unfamiliar object in some familiar place can all trigger the defence mechanism. The horse may shy, sometimes violently, or even attempt to turn round and run off. Whatever he does, the rider's role is to remain calm *and* understanding and to avoid at all costs the jab in the mouth that might result from a momentary loss of balance. Such a jab and the discomfort it produces are immediately associated with the object which startled him, and only go to confirm the danger in the horse's mind and to make him even more nervous.

The Greek general Xenophon, whose work was the inspiration for the classical Masters of the Renaissance, proffered sound advice. It has stood the test of time and is just as relevant today as it was in his lifetime over 2,000

Horses, particularly young ones, shy instinctively from unfamiliar objects and certainly from sudden noises.

years ago: 'When the horse suspects some object and is unwilling to approach, you must make it clear that there is nothing to be afraid of ... and if this fails you must yourself touch the object and lead him up gently. Those who compel the horse with blows make him more frightened than ever.'

There is nothing in Xenophon's prolific writings to suggest that the Ancient Greeks had the sort of affection for the horse which is the endearing hallmark of the British, but they were horsemen and horsemasters.

I reiterate that high feeding and peak fitness levels accentuate the natural defensive instincts and for that reason one has to be prepared to sit tight on fit, fresh horses first thing on a frosty morning. Let Xenophon have the last word: 'Never lose your temper in dealing with horses; this is the one best precept and custom in horsemanship.'

Pain tolerance

It is reasonable to assume that horses and other animals without predatory instincts are likely to be more sensitive to pain than predators and will, in consequence, have a lower pain tolerance. Certainly this seems to be the case with horses, particularly when the species is compared with man's long-standing companion, the dog.

A terrier on hearing the rustle in the hedgerow does not run away. His reaction is to raise his hackles, bare his teeth and attack what to him might be legitimate prey or a natural enemy. Even the adorable, cuddly bundle who seeks by infiltration to make a place for himself under the eiderdown is by nature a killer. He will go down an earth in pursuit of a fox and will possibly get mauled in the process. He comes out scarred and bleeding but still screaming defiance and anxious to tackle his adversary again. He will get into the odd fight; will lick his wounds for a day or two, and will in no way be deterred from picking a quarrel again.

Not so the horse. Stallions will employ threatening behaviour, but a serious fight is unusual and only very rarely will a horse attack a man. The only possible exceptions are horses close to the primitive foundation, like the Asiatic Wild Horse (*Equus Przewalskii* Poliakov) and the Tarpan of the steppes (*Equus Przewalskii* gmelini Antonius). The latter, in wild form, has been extinct for over a hundred years but exists in 'reconstituted' form, as a result of back-breeding by Polish authorities. Both are notably more aggressive than other equines. They are constitutionally strong, fertility rates in the wild are high and they are not prone to sickness of any kind. Any wounds that are sustained heal with remarkable speed and without outside intervention.

The low pain tolerance of most horses, combined with the deeply ingrained flight instinct, can be regarded – and not unreasonably – as the source of some very common rider failings. Nothing is more destructive to the rider/horse partnership than the heavy-handed rider who provokes an unedifying tug-of-war with the unfortunate horse. Bold, courageous horses can it is true become strong in their desire to get on, and that is when the need for a sympathetic, educated hand becomes paramount. If, on the other hand, the rider saws and pulls, we get into that situation when the horse is described as 'fighting the bit' – the horse, you will note, not the rider – and may even be said to be 'bolting'.

The horse is not fighting the bit; he is, in fact, running away from it and the discomfort which he experiences. *The more the rider pulls the greater becomes the need to escape the pain.* The horse's reaction to force is to pull even harder. To the human it seems very illogical when we know that if he slowed down or stopped, that would be the solution to his problem. But viewed with an understanding of the horse's nature, the matter takes on quite the opposite complexion.

Sensitivity

Even a superficial study of the horse's non-predatory instincts indicates the possession of a high degree of sensitivity that will respond to external stimuli.

In fact, it is largely, though not entirely, because of this innate quality – not unconnected with the level of pain tolerance – that we are able to obtain obedience and exert control over an animal ten times our size and immeasurably more powerful.

Because of his sensitivity, the horse learns how to respond to the signals made by hands, legs, body-weight and whip. If, for example, we stand at the horse's head facing the rear and then tap his flank ever so gently with the long whip he will move his quarters *away* from the tapping whip, never towards it. In time he learns to move away from the action of the single leg, if, of course, it is applied in the right place and in proper measure.

In the same manner the acute sensitivity of his mouth allows us to teach response to the action of the bit.

However, there is a line between *submission* and *induced resistance* which is perhaps insufficiently appreciated. The stimulus given by a light pressure on those parts of the mouth on which the bit acts produces *submission*, the horse withdrawing, or giving, in his mouth in response to the action. Nonetheless, there is a point in the scale of the intensity of the action beyond which *submission* is replaced by *resistance*, the very opposite to what was required. It occurs when the hand is insufficiently refined and resorts to force. It is then that we enter the destructive 'you-pull-me-and-I'll-pull-you' syndrome because of the horse's natural inclination to escape discomfort.

Indeed, any heavily applied aid, whether of the seat or the legs, is always more likely to be counter-productive than otherwise.

Memory

Like the elephant, the horse never forgets. The memory is extraordinarily retentive but it can be something of a two-edged sword, for the horse remembers the bad experience just as well as the good ones. As a wise horse-master said: 'In our dealings with him, we write on stone and what is written remains, for better or worse, forever.' Nonetheless, we make use of the memory in every aspect of the horse's training alongside a system of repetition and reward – indeed, we have no alternative but to do so.

Occasionally, it is necessary to correct a misdemeanour, to remind the young horse of his manners, but we need to be absolutely sure that the horse associates the correction with the offence and that the former is administered as nearly simultaneously as it can be. *The horse is incapable of reason.* His memory is long and retentive, certainly, but he is only able to associate cause and result that are closely related in terms of time. (It is held by some students of animal behaviour that there is a limited power of reason. However, it can be argued that 'reason' may be confused with repetitive acts leading to a conditioned response or reaction that may become habitual. The danger in attempting to relate human qualities to those of an animal is that we may begin to slide, if ever so slightly, into expecting a human response from the latter and so risk the descent into anthropomorphosis.)

If a horse kicks at a dog – a heinous offence – or even if he kicks at the spur or the application of the leg – which is also to be discouraged – retribution, in the form of a smart thwack and a growl of disapproval, should be instantaneous, the whip landing almost before his hoof returns to the ground. That, he understands, but if he is taken back to his box and thumped for it ten minutes later he is confused, fearful and becomes sour and resentful.

(No one, of course, would treat a horse like that. Or wouldn't they? I once knew of a horse being treated in that fashion after the completion of a disastrous jumping round – and by a girl, too. Being unfamiliar with Xenophon she simply lost her temper – and so did I.)

I expect that horses can be trained through the fear of punishment, but the system in which reward plays a major part is far more satisfying and productive. Nor is it necessary for the reward to be edible. The horse responds just as well to a pat and an encouraging word. Indeed, reward is at the base of equestrian theory in the sequence of aids which can be summarized as: *Prepare – Act – Yield*. The *preparatory* aid warns of a request about to be made; the aid is then applied and acts; the horse responds and the aid *yields*, *rewarding* the horse for his compliance. Horses really do like to please, if we give them a chance and remember the manners taught at our mother's knee – 'Say *please* and *thank you*'.

The Senses

Finally, we have to consider the senses which complete the horse's personality. There are five of them, along with what may be described as heightened perception, which some would regard as a *sixth sense*.

Taste

The sense of taste may not have too much relevance to training but it is a valuable marketing tool for feed manufacturers and, increasingly, bit makers.

One maker of polyurethane mouthpieces has apple-flavoured bits and certainly most horses relish succulents like apples and carrots, while quite a lot decline the traditional sugar lump and some make it clear that molasses is not to their taste.

The current bitting argument is that horses are encouraged to salivate and therefore relax the jaw as a result of the taste of certain metals. There are some extravagant claims for metals like copper and iron, but they have not been substantiated scientifically. One manufacturer using golden, oxidized metals claims that these metals 'produce the distinctive and pleasant taste that horses love ...' How on earth does he know that?

A long time ago, horsemen used leather mouthpieces and even wrapped the bit in a syrup-soaked bandage to encourage salivation. It was very messy and probably unnecessary. On account of the mess I would not recommend the practice, but if a young horse 'mouths' a copper bit or any other and salivates as a result that is sufficient reason for using it, so long as one is sure that the overall construction is suitable.

Regarding taste in general, horses will seek out herbs, in particular, chicory, but I have one who will have nothing to do with garlic – perhaps out of consideration for his owner – or with worming powders mixed with his feed, however cunningly they may be introduced.

Touch

Taste may not be too much of a consideration but that is by no means the case with the sense of touch, which is inherent in the sophisticated language of the horse and very relevant to the domestic state.

Mutual grooming, particularly in the sensitive area of the withers, creates a relationship between the participants and is noticeable between mares and foals, while stallions use it to stimulate mares sexually. Not surprisingly, this scratching of the withers is just as much appreciated when performed by humans.

Touch is, indeed, a basic form of communication and a way of establishing a relationship. Regular grooming of the horse is an important factor in gaining the horse's confidence, particularly when it is done with the bare forearms in the manner of a massage.

Horses touch new or strange objects with their noses, when the sense of smell is also involved, and they will frequently touch a pole on the ground with a hoof before stepping over it.

Touch, of course, is much involved in riding the horse and teaching

This form of mutual grooming creates a relationship between the participants.

below Horses will frequently touch new or strange objects as a means of accepting their presence.

obedience to the legs. Long ago and from practical experience, I learned that to repeat and intensify the leg aid when there has been no response to the first action of the leg will not produce the required result. More pressure, applied with greater frequency, only deadens the receptor cells on the body. (Dr Marthe Kiley-Worthington, in *The Behaviour of Horses*, wrote of the receptor cells, which are properly termed *nocioceptors*, that they became 'less responsive if the stimulus [the leg pressure] is repeated at intervals of less than about 30 seconds.') Thus the lighter the aid and the shorter the time in which it is active, the more effective it becomes, a matter revisited later in respect of early mounted training. For the time being, suffice it to say that continual kicking with legs and heels is the surest way to make the horse wholly unresponsive. It is also, as my old instructor used to say, 'Such bad manners'.

One hopes that the stupidity of cutting off a horse's muzzle whiskers for none other than cosmetic reasons is now more generally recognized. Whiskers, indeed, serve a useful practical purpose. They are used to touch and evaluate objects out of the horse's vision, particularly the contents of his manger, and then to relay messages to the brain. To cut them off is to deprive the horse of a natural facility and that is neither kind nor sensible.

Smell

Smell, too, plays an important part in the equine language of communication and it is without doubt highly developed, far, far more so than our own.

Foals recognize their dams instantly by smell. Members of a herd group identify each other by what may be a corporate odour given off as pheromones produced by the skin glands. It has a significant role in sexual behaviour, too, the pheromone given off by a mare in oestrus, for example, is a clear indication of her readiness to mate. Noticeably, stallions scent-mark their territory with urine and faeces and will urinate over the excreta of mares within the group to proclaim that they are under their protection.

It is also suggested that the pronounced homing instinct found in horses is in some way connected with the sense of smell, familiar surroundings being associated with a particular scent.

Clearly, too, the sense of smell is a part of the complex defensive system: horses, given that the wind is favourable, picking up the scent of a predator well before he comes into view.

There is no doubt that horses associate their humans with their body odours. Moreover, I am certain that they detect the scent of fear or

Smell is one of the senses and horses use it to recognize their companions and their human leaders. In this case the horse seems to find reassurance in the contact.

nervousness and react accordingly, usually by becoming nervous themselves. (I have it on the best authority, that of a Dyak tracker, who could trail a man in thick jungle by his scent, that humans give off a recognizable fear odour. Members of the old Horseman's Society, a sort of freemasonry of waggoners, horse-keepers, carters and so on, knew all about this too. They used aromatic oils to calm and tame the vicious horses of their day and to obtain their submission. Who knows, perhaps there is something in the modern practice of aromatherapy for horses.)

Hearing

The horse's hearing is a sense far more developed than our own and the range of hearing is probably greater than we imagine.

(Once, when I was unwise enough to write for a 'pop' publishing company, I suggested that horses could detect sound – like the galloping of a distant group of horses or the rumble of a squadron of tanks – through vibrations in the ground transmitted upwards through the feet. My editor, a pro-active young lady, trained in the tabloid field and having scant respect for the niceties of syntax or accuracy, seized upon it with enthusiasm. She re-wrote the piece in sensational tabloid style under the heading 'They Hear with Their Feet'. I had the original text restored and the young lady has never dared alter a comma of mine since.)

The horse's ears not only give expression to the face but provide unmistakable and valuable indications of the horse's state of mind at a given moment. Controlled by no less than thirteen pairs of muscles, the ears are enormously mobile and are capable of being rotated virtually through 360 degrees; while the head itself serves as a remarkably efficient sound box.

It is notable that the horse's ears operate in conjunction with the eyes. When one ear pricks forward, the appropriate eye looks to the front to focus on the object that has attracted attention: when both ears are pricked forward, both eyes are being focused simultaneously. The closer the ears are placed together the better will be the horse's forward vision capability. However, if the horse who is being worked should prick the ears in that

Figure 12. Ear Language:
Left – 'Flies at nine o'clock' – one ear detects the possible attack.

Right – focusing to the front, both ears pricked, eyes similarly focused.

Figure 13. *Top left –* relaxation; *top right –* anger/irritation; *right –* one ear flicked back as when paying attention to rider.

fashion, usually raising the head at the same time, he is distracted from the work in-hand and has stopped listening to his rider.

Ears are lowered and become more flaccid when the animal is dozing and relaxed. They are laid flat back to express displeasure, temper, extreme irritation or aggression, the action often being accompanied by the animal showing the white of the eye. When one ear is stuck out sideways its owner is checking out the presence of a fly or wasp.

Not surprisingly, the horse is exceptionally responsive to the voice and because of the sensitivity of his hearing does not like the high-decibel variety – it makes him nervous. Horses are able to interpret the *tone* of the voice, whatever the words employed, and they can also be taught a limited vocabulary, although they are less receptive in this respect than the dog.

Certainly, the voice is the first and most important of the natural aids in the system of communication. It can soothe, settle and reassure the uneasy ones; check the flighty ones; command the attention of the inattentive; liven the sluggard; encourage, praise and rebuke. What more can you ask?

Sight

Equine sight is unusual in all sorts of respects and quite different from human vision. One the whole we do not appreciate its idiosyncrasies, nor do we relate it adequately enough to the training process.

The equine eye is large in comparison to that of many other animals, pigs and elephants for example. This suggests that the horse relies heavily upon the sense of sight, far more so than those two animals. It is the size of the eye that increases both acuity and the field of vision. Usually, an eye of this size is associated with nocturnal animals or those living in the sort of reduced light found in thick, jungle conditions.

The horse is not nocturnal but he can see pretty well in the dark, far better than humans. Indeed, if one's nerve allows, it is possible to ride fast in the dark and even to jump small obstacles.

Unlike humans and most other animals, the horse focuses on objects largely by raising and lowering the head. The further away the object, the greater will be the degree of elevation required. Obviously, this is a consideration when the horse is being schooled to jump but the focusing mechanism is dependent upon more than the freedom of the head. In fact, it is just as much concerned with the placement of the eye on the head and particularly the width of the forehead; additional contributory factors are related to the width and length of the face and the manner in which the head is 'set on' to the neck. It is generally accepted that, because of the structure of the head, the horse is unable to see the contents of a manger placed at chest height and almost certainly does not see his feet, at least when standing square.

Heavy, common-bred horses and the early 'primitives', like the Asiatic Wild Horse, have the eyes placed more to the side of the head than otherwise because of their usually broad foreheads. This allows for wide *lateral* vision but is restrictive of frontal vision. For the riding horse this is clearly an undesirable conformational feature and a serious disadvantage if the animal is expected to jump. The riding horse who is closer in conformation to the Thoroughbred enjoys far superior frontal vision because the narrower conformation of the forehead is such that the eyes are placed more to the front of the head rather than to the side, an essential attribute for the jumping horse.

Overall, horses have an all-round vision capability and it is possible that in certain circumstances they can see something of the rider on their backs. For myself, I prefer a horse to look to his front when approaching a fence rather than spend time trying to look at me. To obtain a clear sight of a fence, however, involves adjusting the head position and this will be made more difficult if the movement is restricted by martingales and so on, or, of course, the *rider's hand*.

Given that the horse has the required freedom of his head, he sees a fence three strides away (about 13.5 m, or 45 ft) quite clearly with both eyes. At about 1.2 m (4 ft) away his own head prevents him from having a clear view with *both* eyes. If he tips his head a little to the side he can see with *one* eye, otherwise he is 'jumping blind'. Jumping a low hurdle at speed is not quite the same since the leap is made well before reaching the 1.2 m (4 ft) zone. It is very likely that over a 1.5 m (5 ft) fence most horses are jumping blind at the last moment. At that point it is not of much consequence and horses

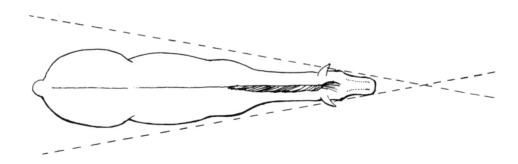

Figure 14. The field of vision, simply expressed.

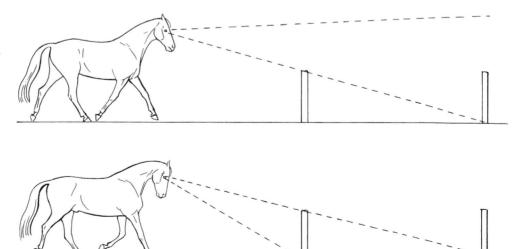

Figure 15. The position of the head as it affects vision.

learn to judge the approach and take-off to the obstacle through experience and training.

Interestingly, the diagrams make it clear that the 'domestic outline' imposed on horses limit the frontal vision quite significantly. Just what, one wonders, can the dressage horse see if he is allowed to become 'overbent', a term implying that the head is inclined behind the vertical plane with the highest point of the neck being some two-thirds up its length instead of at the poll.

The 'Sixth Sense'

Just what is the sixth sense and how it is made evident is a matter for conjecture. Let us call it a 'heightened perception' and accept that it does exist in the equine species.

There are many stories of horses that relate uncharacteristic behavioural reactions to places where tragedies occurred in time long past, and just as many about headless horsemen and headless horses, too!

What is certain is that horses are far better equipped to read the human than the other way round. They sense immediately timidity, hesitation, irritability, courage, confidence and a whole lot more – and they react accordingly.

Nothing is truer than the saying that the horse is a mirror of the rider. Bold riders make for bold horses and I can affirm from experience that bold horses can at least give their riders the reputation for boldness. I think it follows that there are no problem horses, only problem people.

Whether their heightened perception can extend to their being telepathic has never been established unequivocally. However, horses (and perhaps more noticeably ponies, who are on the whole quicker in picking up an atmosphere and sensing the human requirement than their bigger kinsfolk), can respond very accurately to minimal movement.

My daughter's first pony was a little Welshman, sharp as a needle and almost too bright for his own good. So obviously did he enter into the fun of working that I used to give schooling demonstrations with him – or it may have been the other way around. A proper little showman, he jumped fences and went through the school movements, loose and working to quietly spoken works of command, all the time flicking his long eyelashes at the audience. Indeed, he acquired quite a vocabulary to cover our activities together, a most useful accomplishment as he and I taught children to ride. Our *piece de resistance* was when he circled the school loose at walk, trot or canter without a vocal command. I would then ask the audience to *think* hard on the single word 'Whoa' while picturing in their minds the pony coming to a square halt from canter at a particular point on the circle.

He always obliged exactly where I had said he would – but it had nothing to do with the audience, although they always concentrated very hard. He halted because he picked up the very slight relaxation of my body posture. He was sensitive enough to detect that minimal movement, which had, of course, been made previously in his schooling in conjunction with the vocal command.

He taught me as much as any instructor who had the misfortune to count me among his pupils.

PART 2

Facilities and Equipment

Facilities

The possession of comprehensive facilities does not in itself guarantee the quality of the end product, but it does, of course, make the job of training the young horse that much easier to accomplish.

In perfection, the ideal would be a fully equipped equestrian centre with outside all-weather arenas, jumping areas, including an enclosed jumping lane, a cross-country course and even an indoor school. As well, of course, as stabling, turn-out paddocks and easy access to good hacking country and bridlepaths. In reality, most of us will have to manage with something less than that, although there are basic requirements to be met.

Time, for example, is an important consideration and governs the progress that can be made within the duration of the training period. The more time that can be devoted to the training of the young horse in terms of short sessions on a daily basis the more satisfactory will be the outcome. *It is not something to be undertaken at weekends with perhaps an odd hour thrown in during the week as a bonus.*

As a minimum requirement, over and above adequate stabling and a well-fenced paddock, one needs an enclosed schooling area not less than 40 x 20 m, the size of a dressage arena. This allows room for the correct execution of the school exercises and figures. However, the arena does need to be well-drained and to have a good surface so that it is usable in most weather conditions.

In the school area a variety of simple jump equipment is needed. Foremost is an adequate supply of ground-poles and a complement of blocks that can be set to carry poles at varying heights from about 25 cm (10 in) upwards and can be used in the construction of low fences, grids, etc. Otherwise, a couple of sets of uprights and possibly a filler or two is more than adequate.

A trailer or horsebox is an obvious necessity, allowing the young horse to be taken to different venues as a part of his education.

The presence of an older, steady horse is an enormous advantage throughout the training. He can accompany the young horse when out hacking, for example, and sets an example to the youngster in all sorts of ways as well as providing companionship.

Crucial to the making of the young horse is the assistant, and it would be almost impossible to do without one. It is no exaggeration to say that the success of the operation depends very largely upon her efforts (the assistant is usually a 'she').

The ideal is a cheerful, efficient, intelligent and even-tempered person, who is a lightweight, a good rider and totally reliable. She needs to be the sort of person capable of anticipating the need of the moment; who is quiet, quick, economical of speech and able to keep her head in an emergency.

If she meets these criteria, makes the tea and coffee, remembers to switch on the washing machine and is not in the trauma of a love affair, she is a treasure beyond price and will probably not be with you for more than a week, so great will be the demand for her services – and perhaps for her hand, too.

Saddlery and Equipment

A good workman does not blame his tools, but it is probable that he is only as good as they allow him to be.

Leg Protection

The first essential is a set of exercise/work boots as a protection against accidental knocks. They should cover the leg from the top of the cannon bone to the coronet and should be fitted for every work session. My own choice would be a set of felt polo boots with the fastening set on a band of stout elastic. They certainly give excellent protection but, outside of the game, are not now so easily available.

However, the modern neoprene 'schooling wraps' are just as practical. Neoprene absorbs the shock of a blow and the boots also give a degree of support to the suspensory ligament and superficial tendons. Even more importantly, these boots can be fitted easily, quickly and without any risk of uneven pressure at any point on the leg. Young horses are not endowed with great reserves of patience and the ability to get a set of four boots on in double-quick time, and in the knowledge that the pressure is equal through-out their length, is a big consideration.

Later in the ridden work, when the horse is exercising outside the school, he will need a pair of knee-caps. (I have always used knee-caps when hacking out, as much for my own peace of mind as otherwise. On the one occasion when our young lady forgot to put them on before taking a horse out, the poor chap slipped up on a badly-cambered corner and went down on his knees. He was off work for a fortnight and very unhappy. If you look carefully you can still see the scars. They serve as an awful reminder of the sins of omission.)

In the trailer or horsebox it is wise to wrap him up again in travelling boots that extend from above the knee to below the coronet in front, and from above the hock behind, again giving protection around the coronet against a 'tread' made by the opposite foot.

Lungeing Equipment

Work on the lunge (discussed in Part 3) is integral to the training of the young horse and the success of the exercise depends to a degree on the trainer having the right equipment.

Lunge Cavesson

The first requirement is a lunge cavesson. These are easily obtainable and the majority are not much good, being desperately outdated by about 400 years. They are made, one suspects, without the manufacturer being very clear about their purpose.

The cheapest are made from floppy nylon, allowing the all-important nose-plate to droop on the nostrils. Those made from padded web are much better, even if the colour is somewhat garish. The best, in my view and experience, is the lightweight, leather one, well-padded under the metal nose-piece; and even then some minor alterations are needed if it is to fulfil its purpose effectively.

Central to the design of the cavesson is the nose-plate and almost every modern pattern continues to perpetuate the anachronism of the three rings. Some 400 years ago, the two outer rings were placed further to the rear, where they projected outwards, virtually at right angles. The general practice of the time was to fit a rein (the *false* rein) to the outer rings so that one could ride from the cavesson preparatory to transferring control to the bit rein. The horse was, indeed, being 'mouthed' from his nose. (Horses drawing the *fiacre-type* vehicles of the Mediterranean countries are frequently driven from just such a cavesson.)

The modern three-ring cavesson is still suitable for one of its intended purposes; that is, to attach the horse between two training pillars by the outside rings, but that is not a practice of much relevance to the average rider of the twenty-first century and the two rings are to all intents superfluous and a prime example of the philosophy, 'We have always made it that way.'

There are people, I suppose, who still lunge horses from the inside ring, but most of us use the centre ring as being more logical and giving greater control. It is also more convenient; one does not have to change the rein over when one changes the circle from the right to the left or vice versa and it allows far greater finesse in the handling of the lunge rein.

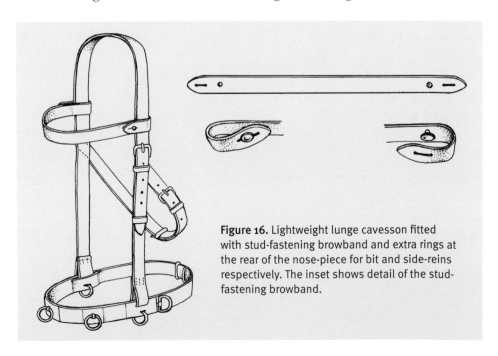

Figure 16. Lightweight lunge cavesson fitted with stud-fastening browband and extra rings at the rear of the nose-piece for bit and side-reins respectively. The inset shows detail of the stud-fastening browband.

It is, indeed, still a sound enough practice to ride off the cavesson preparatory to transferring control to the bit rein, but *not* from side rings which are placed too far forward. For practical purposes and until an intelligently designed cavesson is put on the market, two further dees need to be sewn to the nose-piece, one on each side, to provide an anchorage from which, at the appropriate time, a bit may be suspended. In time side-reins will be fitted directly to the bit and that without having to put on a bridle under the cavesson. Two further rings, fitted above the bit dees, allow the reins to be fastened directly to the cavesson prior to their being attached to the bit and it is then possible for the horse to be ridden from them.

A *properly positioned* jowl strap is necessary to prevent the cavesson being pulled round so that the cheekpiece slides up against the eye. It is sensible never to buy a cavesson until you have the opportunity to fit it to the horse.

A browband is necessary to help keep the headpiece in place and also to get the horse used to the presence of what can be a troublesome piece of the bridle. It causes trouble if it is too short because it pulls the headpiece against the back of the ears. This discomfort distracts the horse and he may well display his irritation by shaking his head. If that is the cause (and there are other causes that encourage persistent head shaking) putting a net over his nose is about as effective as putting one round his tail.

However, since young horses are often a bit apprehensive about having their ears pulled through a bridle-head, it is as well to avoid any unnecessary friction by having a browband fitted with studs (see Figure 16) so that the ends can be passed under and round the headpiece before being turned back and secured to the stud.

Otherwise, the cavesson has to fit snugly if it is to stay in place and that central nose-ring has to be set on a swivel to allow for the movement of the rein.

Lunge Rein and Whip

The cavesson is completed with a lunge rein or line. The best are made from tubular web about 2.5 cm (1 in) or so wide and some 10.6 m (35 ft) long. A swivel fastening prevents the rein from twisting and the best means of attachment is probably a very good quality, lightweight snap hook that can be done up and released quickly. The old buckle fastening is really too cumbersome.

Nylon is not a suitable material for a lunge rein, it is too light and not very pleasant to handle. A lunge line, while not being heavy, does require some weight if the contact between hand and cavesson is to be preserved.

Long-reins for driving can be lighter and the best are the tapered cord or cotton plough lines.

Lunge whips made of fibreglass or nylon are usually well-balanced and very light, both important considerations. A failing is the occasional thong of insufficient length. One does not ever hit the horse with it, but it has to be long enough to touch him below the hocks.

Side-reins

Years ago, in my 'elastic' period, I advocated the use of elastic or rubber inserts in side-reins, as well as on other pieces of equipment. In time I came to realize that I was contributing to that great legion of horses who are perpetually behind the bit (a fault that is also encouraged by riding reins that out of a mistaken kindness and a misunderstanding of equestrian theory are similarly set with elastic).

The so-called 'give and take' action of the elastic side-rein, particularly the 'take' part, encourages evasion since it causes the horse to withdraw the nose and come out of contact with the bit. Today, I advocate the use of a light, plain leather rein with ample adjustment and fastening at the rings of roller and bit with clip hooks.

The use and value of side-reins is generally accepted but the fact that they can be misused is not always sufficiently appreciated. Side-reins are as much involved in the *back to front* philosophy as any other aspect of equestrian theory and practice. The most common example of misuse is when that precept is reversed and the reins are adjusted too tightly as a result.

The shortened adjustment is made in a mistaken effort to *impose* a head carriage (and to do so from *front to back*) instead of the reins being used to help the horse find for himself a head carriage that contributes to his freedom and balance. Whether attached to cavesson or bit, tight, short reins cause the horse to evade this discomfort by retracting his nose and becoming 'behind the bit'. This forced shortening of the front leads to lack of engagement behind, minimal hock flexion and a short, restricted stride made from a stiffened shoulder. Any semblance of a rounded top-line is, of course, lost.

The rational way to use the side-reins is to adjust them in the early stages at almost their full length, when their weight alone will induce a lowering of the head. The object then is to push the horse forward from the whip into the hand until he is lowering his head to make contact with the bit. He is,

Figure 17. Side-reins: properly introduced and adjusted they contribute materially to the balance and rounded outline of the horse.

in effect, *seeking out* the bit, an exercise that is greatly assisted by making use of ground-poles, which will encourage a greater lowering and stretching of the neck, a rounding of the back in response to the stretched cervical ligament and the increased engagement required of the hind legs.

When that has been accomplished the side-reins can be shortened by gradual stages for the trot work on the circle until there is just a slight dip in their centre when the horse is in movement. Used in that fashion the reins conform to the *back to front* precept and can assist materially in producing a balanced carriage while going some way to 'making the mouth', an art that today is in danger of being neglected.

I am not impressed by arguments for the inside rein to be adjusted shorter than its partner in order to enforce a 'bend'. In fact, the 'bend' is no more than a twist at the poll and the horse is very likely to lean on the inside of the bit or retract the nose to evade it. The weight, in consequence, is thrown on the inside shoulder, causing the quarters to be carried outwards and away from the track made by the forefeet – a positive encouragement to crooked movement.

Body Roller

Now, one needs a body roller to which the side-reins can be attached. It is the centre piece of the schooling tackle and a sort of control console. It should be between 11.5–13 cm (4½–5 in) wide. It has to have well-fitted pads and needs to be constructed in two parts to adjust on either side of the body. Three large rings are fitted to each side on the front edge, the lowest being about halfway down the horse's body. These are the attachment points for the side-reins and the centre one can also be used for long-reining. Otherwise, large, fixed rings for the long-reins can be sewn to the roller at the bottom of the pads or panels and this is probably the preferable arrangement. A further ring, on a short adjustable strap, is fitted between the panels at the forward edge, to be used when side-reins are finally fitted at hand height. Another ring for the crupper is fastened to the rear edge between the two panels. Finally, a large ring is built into the roller at the centre of the belly girth between the forelegs in case at any point some form of martingale is needed.

Whether or not a breast-girth is necessary is a matter on which trainers differ. The pro-lobby claim that it eliminates the necessity to girth the roller tightly and, of course, that it prevents that item from slipping back. As a member of the indifferent lobby I see no reason for not girthing firmly enough to hold the roller in place. The horse soon accepts the pressure if the girthing is carried out gradually. In any event, it is just as likely, because of the shape of the young horse, for the roller to move forward and the crupper will take care of that. In fact, a further use of the roller is to accustom the horse to tension around the barrel and is a common-sense preparation for the fitting of saddle and girth. (To this end it can be left in place in the stable for short periods to familiarize the horse with the feel of the girth round his body.)

A well-made roller with the panels shaped to avoid pressure on the spine should fit like a saddle and lie securely behind the trapezius muscle. The multiplicity of rings allows the side-reins to be moved gradually upwards from the lowest position until they approximate to the position of the rider's hands when the horse is under saddle.

The belly girth fits into the sternum curve (the indentation behind the chest), which is effectively the equivalent of the human waist. Properly fitted, the roller then inclines a little to the rear of the vertical and if the belly band is shaped back at its front edge there will be no chance of it chafing behind the elbows. All in all, this pattern, with the addition of a crupper, is a roller to meet all eventualities.

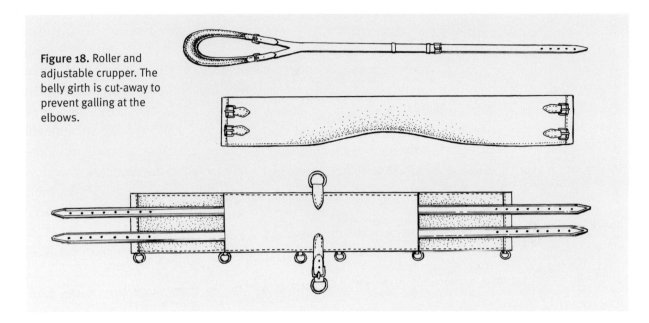

Figure 18. Roller and adjustable crupper. The belly girth is cut-away to prevent galling at the elbows.

Crupper

There was a time when I discouraged the use of a crupper because I thought it might encourage a hollowing of the back, which in certain patterns of breaking tackle it did. But I would now argue that properly fitted, more loose than tight, it has a notable effect on the overall carriage, encouraging the horse to use the loins, without exerting anything but the lightest tension on the dock. Used with the side-reins, adjusted to hang in a slight loop, it does help to 'bring the horse together' in a balanced outline. Moreover, its use helps the horse to accept what I term handling-by-equipment-contact.

Initially, the horse may give a hump or two, clamping down his tail and stiffening through his back at the unfamiliar feel of the crupper under his dock, but within minutes he will be going quite happily and a very useful lesson in submission has been taught and learnt.

For easy fitting the crupper needs to be adjustable on either side of the dock. When in place it should be possible to insert an upright hand between the back strap and the back.

Of course, there are cruppers and cruppers. The best is made of soft leather stuffed with linseed. The heat of the body, combined with the application of a cleaning grease and the linseed itself, makes the whole wonderfully soft and pliable. It is important that it should be so, for if the dock should become rubbed and sore we may expect the horse to feel uncomfortable and react accordingly.

I have come across more than one DIY crupper made from a length of rubber hose well-wrapped in a soft bandage, and they appeared to do the job wonderfully well.

(Interestingly, the use of the tail in schooling and working horses is of long standing. It crops up again and again in the methods employed by the old horse-tamers and, indeed, those of the ancient horse-peoples.)

Bit

Very important is the choice of bit, and opinions differ widely on which is most suitable.

Many experienced folk, particularly those of an older generation, cling to the old type, conventional mouthing bit, either in the straight bar or jointed form, with 'keys' set in the centre of the mouthpiece. The theory is that the horse plays with the keys, an action inducing salivation and, one hopes, a relaxation of the lower jaw. It is not an unreasonable supposition but there is no doubt that the act of mouthing can cause a retraction of the head, so that the horse comes 'behind the bit'. Moreover, I am by no means convinced that the horse is not encouraged to put his tongue over the bit, which is a habit difficult to break. Once the tongue is over the bit it is quite impossible for the horse to respond to the hand and any hope of a civilized dialogue between the two is at once negated.

My own choice is for a polyurethane straight bar bit with a 'wavy' mouthpiece and an apple flavour! That does very well in the introductory stages and when the time comes to take a step further I would use either a German ported snaffle, allowing room for the tongue, or my old favourite, the Fulmer or Australian loose-ring cheek snaffle, the choice depending on the conformation of the mouth.

Later in the training it may be necessary to introduce one or other of the corrective/supportive nosebands like a Flash or something similar. At the outset, however, a plain cavesson as part of a conventional snaffle bridle is sufficient.

However, great attention has to be paid to the fitting of the bridle. Bits that are too large or too small create their own horrendous problems and skimped browbands and throatlatchs both cause discomfort and understandable resistances.

Since throughout the schooling period and, indeed, beyond, the mouth should be inspected, or at least checked over, on a daily basis, it is no bad plan to keep a Swales pattern veterinary gag (Figure 19) to hand. The horse will be taught to accept his mouth being opened by the tactful use of finger and thumb easily enough, but should a more thorough inspection be necessary the Swales gag is a simple device that is easily operated and one that horses generally accept with equanimity.

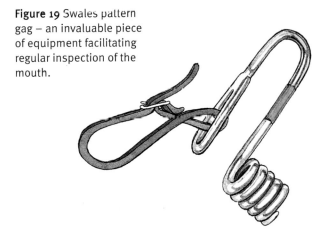

Figure 19 Swales pattern gag – an invaluable piece of equipment facilitating regular inspection of the mouth.

Saddle

The saddle is a major item of equipment and increasingly it is the product of innovative technology directed at ensuring near-perfect fit and balance. Manufacturers now recognize that the saddle contributes materially to the horse's comfort and freedom of movement, as well as to the performance potential of both horse and rider. Indeed, it is my belief that the design and construction of the best modern saddles is often somewhat in advance of the rider's ability to use them to the greatest advantage.

Of course, there is a problem with young horses who are growing and changing shape as they develop, and it is perhaps for this reason that so many people used to use an old saddle in the early stages of ridden work regardless of the niceties of fit or how well it positioned the rider. (Mothers with growing children will appreciate the difficulty more than most.) In fact, just as it is essential that a child's shoes are properly fitted, so it is very necessary to use a saddle that allows for the young horse's muscular development and overall growth. (Indeed, over time, these criteria may dictate the need for more than one saddle.) The saddle used must be in no way restrictive of the horse's movement and it has also to position the rider in balance.

Damage done by a badly-fitting saddle in the early years of the horse's life can be the source of back problems and restricted movement in the mature animal. At that point, it is quite unreasonable to expect that the purchase of a new and probably expensive saddle will effect a cure. Mind you, in this litigious age it will not stop some owners from blaming the saddle and the saddler for the horse's deteriorating performance.

My advice is to purchase one of the synthetic saddles in which to start off the three-year-old. They are well-designed and constructed, the best are adjustable to the changing conformation of the back and they are priced very competitively. Choose a model that is not too dipped in its seat – you may wish to bale out quickly or be given no alternative but to take that course – *and have it fitted by a qualified saddle-fitter.*

If, a year or eighteen months later, you aspire to a state-of-the-art, designer saddle, you can do so in the knowledge that the condition of the horse's back will present no fitting problems.

Other than this, always use one of the modern, slim-line protective saddle cloths or numnahs. Have the saddle fitting checked regularly and bear in mind that if the saddle is out of balance it is more likely to be on account of your riding than anything else.

Ancillary Equipment

A long whip, of dressage length, is an essential tool and no trainer should be without one. Its purpose is to reinforce the action of the leg if necessary but it also serves to refine the response to the leg aid. When schooling from the ground, as when teaching the walk, etc., it becomes, in effect, an extension of the rider's hand. You can't do without one.

A simple lead rein is another necessity. It can be made from a soft, plaited cotton rope with a snap hook fastening, or from tubular or padded web, the whole being about 2.4 m (8 ft) long.

In the risk-conscious climate of the twenty-first century, handlers should always wear a hard hat and use a pair of gloves when either leading or, more particularly, lungeing. Gloves give one a better purchase on the rein and should the horse take off, pulling the rein through the hand, they will prevent a painful burn.

Additional Training Aids

The mail-order catalogues are replete with schooling equipment over and above the basic requirement. On the whole, these devices have no part to play in the training programmes of the three- and four-year-old horse, although some may be useful in subsequent schooling. They are included here with explanations of their purpose and action in case, at some later date, readers may consider using one or other of them, perhaps as a means of correction. At that point it is advisable to understand the pros and cons of the device one intends to use and my explanations are probably more reliable than the claims made by the catalogue copy writers.

Chambon

In most European countries the Chambon is regarded as being part of the lunge equipment, although it is not in general use in Britain nor, I think, in America. It is, nonetheless, a very useful tool, epitomizing that inescapable Gallic logic that has contributed so much to equestrian thinking.

Its purpose is to cause a lowering of the head and neck, a raising of the shoulder, a rounding of the back and, of course, the engagement of the hind legs under the body.

Initially, it is best to work the horse loose in an enclosed space, adjusting the cords so that the action only comes into play when the head is carried unduly high. Subsequently the equipment can be tightened gradually, a little by little each day, until the poll is carried in line with the withers and the nose on a level with the hip. Encouraged by the indications of the whip, the horse will then begin to move in the short, rhythmical trot which is characteristic of the device and the most rewarding in terms of balance and muscular development.

Once the horse accepts the Chambon one can use it with the lunge rein but never for more than for about ten to fifteen minutes.

Within the training programme recommended here the Chambon is perhaps best viewed as a top-up aid, used to give additional emphasis to the usual lunge work that is carried out over poles and in side-reins, or to act as a corrective.

Figure 20. The Chambon, operated with tact, will certainly contribute to the outline, encouraging a short, rhythmical trot that helps to build the muscles correctly.

Figure 21. Detail of the Chambon indicating the general areas of pressure and the resultant lowering of the head.

De Gogue

While the use of the Chambon is confined to the lunge exercises, the de Gogue can be used both for the lunge and ridden work. On that account it can be viewed as an extension of the principles inherent in the Chambon, but in essence it has to be regarded, as its designer, Rene de Gogue, intended, as a complete *system* within itself.

The device is certainly more precise and refined than the Chambon in its action and is capable, in educated hands, of producing far wider-ranging effects. It is based on the recognition of what de Gogue terms 'the three points of major resistance' (defined as mouth, poll and base of neck) in the unschooled or badly schooled horse. My personal view is that its use is best reserved for the post-four-year-old training period or, at least, towards the end of that period. There is just a possibility that a less than experienced rider, or even a good rider using the de Gogue for the first time and not being familiar with the restraints it imposes, might work the horse to a point where the muscles begin to ache, a condition that is always to be avoided. In fact, it is surprising how easily the horse can be over-ridden in the early lessons using the de Gogue.

To break down stiffness (de Gogue's words) in the three designated 'areas of resistance' the device is fitted to form a triangle between the three points. Quite quickly, the horse learns to carry the head in the required lower position within the confines imposed. This is the 'independent' position and the one retained in the early ridden work. Once more, the greatest benefit is gained by working the horse loose in this position before using the de Gogue on the lunge.

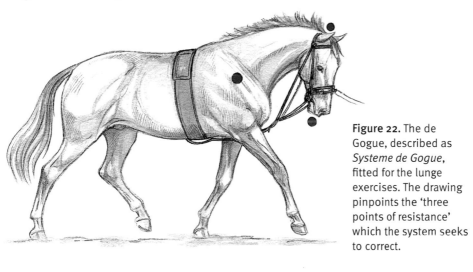

Figure 22. The de Gogue, described as *Systeme de Gogue*, fitted for the lunge exercises. The drawing pinpoints the 'three points of resistance' which the system seeks to correct.

Figure 23. The de Gogue fitted in the 'independent' position with the addition of a riding rein. The drawing indicates the general area of pressure and the consequent lowering of the head.

Used tactfully, the apparatus raises the base of the neck, giving greater freedom to the shoulder. At the same time there is a noticeable engagement of the hocks and greater flexion of the hock joints. The whole contributes very materially to the muscular development of a rounded top-line and there is far greater flexion (reduction of resistance) in the poll than would be possible with the Chambon. Gradually, poll flexion will be encouraged further, as well as the nose being brought inwards, but this only comes about if the horse is made to move forward freely and with notable energy. (The 'stops' fitted to the rein just below the small pulley on the poll pad ensure that the horse does not become overbent, a vitally important consideration.)

The de Gogue, in company with other devices, will not effect a transformation of itself; it needs a little positive, intelligent help from the operator.

The next stage in the system is for the horse to be ridden with the martingale (the de Gogue does, indeed, belong to that family) in the same 'independent' position, but with the addition of an extra rein to the bit ring.

Initially, the adjustment needs to be loosened until the horse is used to the weight on his back and is moving actively in response to the rider's legs. When that has been accomplished the adjustment can be gradually tightened again.

Finally, the rein is attached directly to the cords in the 'direct' position, the triangle then being completed by the rein going straight to the hand.

Ideally, it is claimed that a horse schooled in this system gives the rider maximum control with minimum effort, while performing with all the athleticism which the correct and supple development of form and musculature makes possible.

Figure 24. The de Gogue in its 'direct' position controlled by the rider's hand. The device is only within the province of the advanced rider and is NOT for the novice.

That is the object and it is possible to achieve if the rider is sufficiently skilful and the schooling has not been hurried. Otherwise, I do not think it comes within the province of the less accomplished rider. Indeed, even for the more competent it is best used under the initial supervision of an experienced instructor. However, in the hands of a skilled rider who is familiar with it, the de Gogue can be used not only for schooling on the flat but also for jumping and cross-country.

Figure 25. In the 'direct' position and in the hands of an advanced rider the de Gogue can be used across country and for arena jumping.

The Balancing Rein

Among the welter of reins designed to improve and/or correct the carriage and balance the Abbot-Davies rein stands on its own.

The principle of tail-reining, incorporated in the Abbot-Davies system, has been with us since the Egyptian chariot corps swept through the valley lands of the Tigris and Euphrates 3,000 years ago, and running reins have been about for just as long. Peter Abbot-Davies combined the two in his balancing rein but was careful to mitigate the potentially inhibiting nature of the latter by incorporating an ingeniously engineered 'shock-absorbing' system based on a pulley and a precision built spring.

The declared intention of the balancing rein was to create an effective working outline, employing the forces of the powerful physique to full advantage, by building up the muscles of the neck and back and doing so in a shorter space of time than would be considered possible when employing conventional means.

Once more, the process begins by raising the shoulder and so contributing to its freedom. The back becomes rounded as a result of fully engaged quarters and the horse moves, characteristically, with head and neck lowered and the former strongly flexed.

The rein operates in three positions:

Position 1 entails attachment from mouth to girth by means of a rubber rod via the 'shock-absorber' pulley and spring.

Position 2 calls for an extended connection from mouth to tail by means of a rope under the belly passing through the soft, sheepskin sleeve, again via the shock-absorber.

Position 3 is that used in the lunge exercises and operates from the mouth to behind the poll by means of a rubber connection.

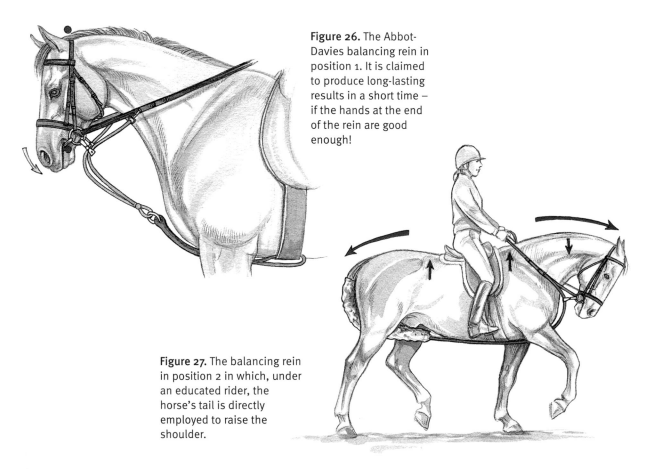

Figure 26. The Abbot-Davies balancing rein in position 1. It is claimed to produce long-lasting results in a short time – if the hands at the end of the rein are good enough!

Figure 27. The balancing rein in position 2 in which, under an educated rider, the horse's tail is directly employed to raise the shoulder.

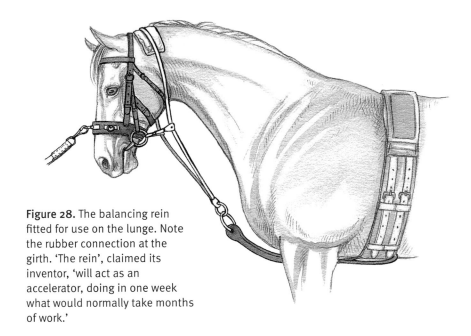

Figure 28. The balancing rein fitted for use on the lunge. Note the rubber connection at the girth. 'The rein', claimed its inventor, 'will act as an accelerator, doing in one week what would normally take months of work.'

In fact, Position 3 can also be used under saddle to produce a temporary but exaggerated lowering of the head and neck that gives greater emphasis to the raised shoulder and encourages maximum possible engagement of the quarters. Used for *short* periods in this way the message to the horse is made abundantly clear and calls for maximum effort on his part.

It is Position 2 that is central to the system and acts to introduce the required rounded outline. Nonetheless, it has to be used sympathetically and only for short periods if the horse is not to be made stiff and sore.

Two fifteen-minute lessons when training begins are sufficient to place the horse in the rounded outline. Otherwise the rein in this position is used as an occasional booster, perhaps just once a month, to re-establish any loss of the rounded form.

For everyday use the rein is fitted in Position 1. This will allow for normal schooling on the flat and for jumping fences of up to 1 m (3 ft 3 in) in height. The effect of the rein, in respect of the outline produced, is retained when the horse is ridden in no more than a snaffle because of the muscular development that has already been established by its use.

'This patent rein', claimed its inventor, a very accomplished horseman, 'will act as an accelerator, doing in one week what would normally take months of work.' Whether that is an appropriate quote to include in a book advocating 'hastening slowly' along a logical training route in which each lesson is a preparation for the one that follows, is arguable.

I do not doubt the truth of Peter Abbot-Davies' assertion when the rein is operated by riders of his own level of competence, but in less experienced hands, accompanied by less than effective driving aids, there are inherent dangers. The mouth to tail position (2), for example, is best attempted initially under the supervision of a skilled trainer, and those contemplating using the rein would be well-advised to take a short course of instruction before becoming involved.

Like the Chambon, and to a degree the de Gogue, the Abbot-Davies rein is 'flattered by imitation' and many of those imitations are not really much more than variations on the side-rein, draw-rein theme. On the whole, they are best avoided even – or perhaps more particularly – when endorsed by the experts.

Bitting and Bending Tackle

In the days of the carriage horse and the big dealing yards, every 'nagsman' worth his salt had his set of bitting harness or bending tackle. Often they depended for their effect on a number of cords being meticulously adjusted to exactly the right tension and the nagging fraternity guarded its secrets jealously.

Devices of this sort worked sufficiently well to present the finished article for sale, but then the nagsmen, many of whom adopted seats that would be quite unacceptable in the twenty-first century, were very skilful, full-time horsemen. Moreover, to a man, or nearly so, they were well-versed in the 'making' of a mouth – a skill not so much in evidence today even at the rarefied heights of advanced equestrian competition.

The modern equivalent of their devices is probably represented by the Pessoa tackle (ennobled in the mail-order catalogues as a 'training system'). It does, indeed, encourage a proper outline, despite the catalogue 'blurb'. It will do no harm and may well do good and it is a convenient tool, but the same result is obtainable with a lunge rein and a pair of long-reins.

The 'Razor in the Monkey's Paw'

Inevitably, every serious rider will come up against the draw- or running-rein, condemned by one of the world's great trainers, the late Bert de Nemethy, who was responsible for the brilliant American teams of the 1950s and 60s, as 'the razor in the monkey's paw'.

The usual aphorism employed is that 'running-reins are for experts and experts don't use them', which is nonsense. Experts do use them, if sometimes inexpertly, but do so on a temporary basis and precious few make any distinction between the two, i.e. the draw-rein and the running-rein.

The *running-rein* is attributed, possibly incorrectly, to the sole English Master, William Cavendish, Duke of Newcastle (1592–1676) and was in general use throughout the most glorious period of 'classical' equitation and for long after in the cavalry schools of Europe. The rein 'runs' from beneath the saddle flap or just below it, through the bit rings and from thence to the rider's hands (in Newcastle's day, it was attached to the cavesson).

Figure 29. 'The razor in the monkey's paw.' There are two versions, the draw-rein (*top*) and the running rein (*below*). Both can result in no more than a shortening of the front end, in contradiction to the dictum 'back to front'.

The *draw-rein* originates at the girth and passes through the forelegs to the bit rings. Of the two it is the more direct and decisive in its action since it 'draws' the head downwards as well as causing the nose to be taken to the rear. The *running-rein* does much the same but places less emphasis on the lowered head. Even less coercion is apparent when the rein is fastened from the chest and then through the bit rings. The rein is used to assist in shortening and rounding the outline and in countering the common tendency to evade working within the frame asked for by legs and hands.

Properly employed it 'suggests' an appropriate head position, but very often it may do nothing more than shorten the front end at the cost of less actively engaged quarters, hence the 'razor in the monkey's paw'.

Applied intelligently, from an active leg aid the horse is pushed into lightly restraining fingers and then, when the horse responds, a few strides can be taken within the imposed frame. Little by little the number of strides is increased. Exactly the same course is taken when riding without the help of the draw-rein; the presence of the subsidiary rein only speeds up the process.

In fact, to be effective the rein needs to be used in conjunction with a second rein attached directly to the bit. The schooling rein is then held 5 cm (2in) shorter than its counterpart. As the horse is pushed forward into the bridle and the bit acts across the bars, control is transferred from the draw-rein to the direct rein. If the horse seeks to evade again the draw-rein can be brought into play once more. So long as the rider is tactful and the legs are active the horse quickly appreciates that submission to the direct rein is more comfortable than otherwise.

Figure 30. A simple form of draw-reins acting on the poll. This will bring the head inwards but is non-productive without active legs and seat.

On the whole, the reins are not approved by national governing bodies other than the German National Equestrian Federation, which gives a cautious approval under 'certain circumstances', and then blows it by quoting horses of an 'extremely difficult conformation' as an acceptable circumstance. Is the Federation condoning the use of coercion to correct a natural physical defect, one wonders?

There is certainly no place for these reins in the rational system of making the three- and four-year-old.

The 'Professor's' Harness

Far less controversial and more productive is that simple piece of equipment known as Galvayne's harness. It is a remarkably effective aid in loading hesitant horses, particularly if one is ever single-handed. It could be used to encourage a young horse to walk or trot in-hand and can be used to deal with the one who continually pulls back against the headcollar when tied up. Anyone dealing with young horses could do worse than keep one handy in the tack room against unforeseen eventualities.

In its simple form, it is just a loop of soft rope passed round the quarters and then up on either side of the body toward the withers. It can be kept in place by a breast rope or any simple arrangement that supports the rope and prevents it from falling to the ground – a basic harness, in fact.

The ends of the rope continue forward and are passed through the bit rings or the side dees of a headcollar. A pull on the rope in front results in a tightening of the loop round the quarters and it causes understandable puzzlement in the equine mind. In short the horse has difficulty in associating the handler in front with the persuasive push experienced at his rear which, in nine cases out of ten, causes him to move forward.

An even more persuasive effect is obtained by passing the rope under the dock or even by knotting it round that part. From personal experience of loading mules into railway wagons and the like, I can vouch for this method as ensuring immediate compliance with the request for forward movement.

The harness is illustrated with variations in 'Professor' Sydney Galvayne's book *The Horse* and this nineteenth-century 'horse-tamer', one of a succession who made lucrative visits to Britain from America, used it to teach the horse to submit to being tied up. In this instance the rope ends were tied to the wall ring and when the horse ran back it received a strong pull on the tail or round the quarters as a result. The horse experienced no pull on the headcollar as he might have expected, nothing broke and instead of

Figure 31. The 'professor's harness', a version of Galvayne's leading harness that is infinitely more affective than devices employing pressure on the head alone.

breaking free, he had inflicted discomfort on himself which he found difficult to understand.

The principle of a psychological force being applied by a mechanical one activated by the horse himself was a sound one and very much part of the tradition of the horse-tamers.

(Sydney Galvayne, who like many of his peers assumed the title of 'Professor', came to Britain from America in 1884, appearing before Queen Victoria at Balmoral in 1887 to demonstrate his 'new, humane and scientific system'. In fact he was not an American, nor was his name Galvayne. He was Australian and his real name was Osborn. Possibly, he changed names because of disputes between himself and his former employer in America, 'Professor' Sample, the inventor of a horse-taming machine!

Galvayne went on to obtain acceptance in the highest veterinary circles of the day, particularly on account of his book *Horse Dentition* which contained a treatise on ageing by examination of the teeth. It involved observation of 'Galvayne's Groove', the name given to the mark appearing on the teeth between ten and twenty years of age, which remains standard practice today.

In the South African War (1899–1902) Galvayne was made Director of Breaking to the Imperial Army in South Africa. As well as the 'groove' he added a new verb to the equestrian vocabulary, 'to galvayne'. It involved tying the head of a recalcitrant subject to his tail to establish the trainer's authority – it is not a part of the Rational Way and is not described in this book.)

PART 3

Primary School

Objectives

The objectives in the weeks of training between April and August (or the corresponding periods to allow for climatic conditions in individual countries) are these:

1. Getting the young horse accustomed to the habit of discipline, which amounts to no more than good manners, and to accept being handled all over his body.

2. Preparing the horse physically to carry weight on his back.

3. Teaching him to accept weight on his back.

4. Him learning how best to carry the weight, which will involve his making adjustments in his balance.

5. Him understanding the rudiments of control through the rider's seat, legs and hands.

In all, but more particularly in the first requirement, we are concerned with the development of a mental outlook, as well as a physical one.

Vocabulary

Additionally in this primary phase the horse will begin to acquire a vocabulary. Horses do not understand human speech but they are exceptionally sensitive to the tone of voice. A low, soothing tone quietens and reassures; a sharp, staccato note calls for immediate, vigorous action or for an increase in the energy displayed. A warning growl is a reprimand and gives notice that the horse should desist from whatever action provoked it.

For all that, it is possible for the horse to acquire a limited vocabulary of imperatives. 'Come here', 'Stand still', 'Open wide' (for looking at the mouth), 'Lift' (for picking up the feet), 'Move over', 'Back' are obvious examples. Mind you, it is quite possible for those of a perverse turn of mind to teach a horse to 'Come here' by saying 'Go away'. It is the association of words and tone with the making of a particular response that is important.

Of course, we can also 'talk' to horses through body-language without opening our mouths. I have already mentioned the pony Muffin, who would halt when I dropped my hands and relaxed my body, and who would jump a designated fence on command but really because my body was so placed that it indicated the fence quite clearly. Circus trainers working 'liberty' horses are adept in the use of body-language, as are many producers and trainers of horses and ponies.

The Guiding Trilogy

Life for the young horse in this primary period of training will be filled with new sights, sounds and experiences. Naturally, he will find the odd occasion that causes him alarm or confusion and he may sometimes react by resisting whatever is being asked of him. Nonetheless, we should never lose sight of the need to work towards producing a state of calm in our pupil and while pussy-footing about is the last thing that is needed we do need to employ methods which, while being positive, are acceptable in that context.

Calm is one of the three commandments contained in the dictum given to us by General L'Hotte, one of France's greatest horsemen: 'CALM, FORWARD, STRAIGHT.' In those words are contained all the principles of rational schooling.

Without being calm, which does not mean half-asleep, the horse will be inattentive, unresponsive and usually disobedient, none of which are conducive to constructive work.

Forward is an essential element in schooling. Most of our problems under saddle derive from a lack of free forward movement, a quality to be encouraged and preserved at almost any cost. Forward movement certainly implies instant and willing obedience to the legs and the indication of the whip, when the horse is being led or lunged, but it is much more than a conditioned physical response. It is, in fact, just as much the manifestation of a mental attitude as of a physical one.

To complete the trilogy, the horse needs to be *straight* if the physical structure is to be used effectively and efficiently. In the simplest terms a horse is said to be straight when the hind feet follow exactly the tracks made by the forefeet. Most young horses are not straight because of an unequal development of muscle on either side of the body or, indeed, because of a natural predisposition to a slight congenital curvature. In that state they move like a Lurcher dog with the hind feet carried to one side of the tracks of the forefeet. In consequence the propulsive thrust of the quarters, instead of being delivered directly to the front, is partly expended by being directed to one side or the other and away from the direction of the movement.

That in itself is important enough, but just as much so is the fact that the rider is able, if the horse is straight, to control the position of the quarters which, if you think about it, control the direction. A horse is quite able to move to the left when his head is bent to the right. (Watch the small child with his pony's nose pulled back almost to the rider's knee while the pony moves determinedly in the opposite direction.) Conversely, *where the*

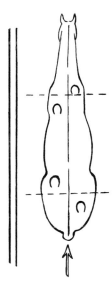

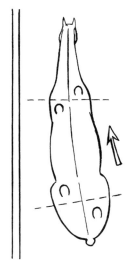

Figure 32. *Left:* the straight horse, hind feet in the track of the forefeet with the thrust of the quarters delivered directly to the front. *Below:* the horse is patently not straight and the thrust of the quarters is out of line.

quarters point, there the horse must go and, unless the rider is able to re-position the quarters, control of the situation passes to the horse.

It is for this reason that, in the secondary stage of schooling, we work towards inducing *mobility* in the quarters so that they can be moved at will by the action of a single leg. In consequence we have the ability to straighten the horse by correcting any unwanted shift of the back end which may be made as an evasion. If your horse goes forwards and you can also control the position of the quarters, it becomes very difficult for him to do other than jump the obstacle at which he is presented. Indeed, it is easier for him to jump than to do otherwise.

Stress

Stress is endemic to both the human and the animal condition and is, indeed, very fashionable in the former. Since it is unavoidable we can only seek to keep it within reasonable bounds.

In fact, a degree of stress is, in itself, not such a bad thing. To achieve anything worthwhile we, and our horses, need to be 'stretched' just a little, otherwise we are reduced to no more than unresponsive dumplings.

Stress in the young horse is contained largely by the exercise of good, common-sense management founded on knowledge and respect.

Physical stress occurs in any form of exertion. It becomes unacceptable and even cruel if a horse is compelled to work beyond the limits of his natural capacity or of his physical condition. Poor, inadequate feeding is also a factor and over-feeding is almost as bad. Additional sources are the presence of an excessive worm-burden and neglected teeth. Badly fitting saddlery is another – along, of course, with incompetent handling and riding.

Mental stress may arise from an interruption to the usual routine and will certainly be present at a low level when the young horse is first brought into work (a bit like the little boy on his first day at school). However, this is rarely long-lasting.

On the other hand every effort should be made to stable a young horse so that he can see and communicate with others or, at the very least, where he can see what is going on in the yard. It really is asking for trouble to put him into what amounts to solitary confinement.

Travelling may present a difficulty with some individuals and, certainly, sudden changes of diet can result in uncharacteristic behaviour.

Diet

In the twenty-first century horse feed is a major equestrian industry, relying increasingly on scientific research in the formulation of products, and supported by qualified nutritionists who are more than ready to advise horse-owners on the use of their products.

The range of feedstuffs available is wide and on that account can cause some confusion. Nonetheless, manufacturers are meticulous in providing information on the outside of the bags and containers and it deserves to be studied carefully.

Otherwise, the long-established principles of feeding still hold good and these are discussed in some detail in Part 4 – Nutrition. At this stage it is sufficient to establish the relevant *bulk/concentrate* ration and the *total food intake* applicable to the individual concerned.

The total food requirement (concentrates plus hay) is estimated at being 3 per cent of the body-weight for young stock and between 2–2.5 per cent for older horses. In practice these figures may prove to be somewhat generous. They would certainly be so for Irish Draughts and for many of the Draught crosses, for Welsh Cobs, Cleveland Bays and ponies. These types are all frugal feeders and good converters of food, whereas those carrying a high percentage of Thoroughbred blood *generally* need to be fed a more generous ration.

In short, horses, like people, vary in their food requirement. Some horses do well on a particular mix, while others thrive not at all. It is all a question of the eye and intuitive feel of the master.

Calculating Weight

The first essential is to establish the weight of the young horse. For many years I employed the following formula and found it to be a reliable basis for calculating the feed requirement:

$$\frac{GIRTH^2 \times LENGTH}{300} = \text{Weight in lb.}$$

The girth measurement is taken in inches round the barrel from just behind the withers through the sternum curve (the girth groove). The square of the girth is obtained by multiplying the figure by itself (i.e. 76 in x 76 in).

Length, also in inches, is measured from a line vertically above the *point of the shoulder* back to the *point of the buttock*.

For the weight to be expressed in kilograms, either convert with a calculator or use this formula (for which you will still need a calculator).

$$\frac{\text{GIRTH (cm)}^2 \times \text{LENGTH}}{8,700} = \text{Weight in kg.}$$

The bother of calculating weight by formula can be avoided by using a calibrated tape measure (weightape), available from feed merchants, saddlers and so on. But take care, they can be wildly inaccurate and I would suggest that they should be checked against the formula before being used on a regular basis.

Having arrived at a figure it would, nonetheless, be unwise to start feeding that quantity straightway unless the horse is already on a ration of similar proportions; far better, as always, to start with a small amount and increase the ration very gradually over 2–3 weeks.

Constituents of Feed

Settle on a low-energy, light work mix supported by something like an alfalfa chaff, a combination that can be made even more palatable by the addition of sliced carrots and apples – the succulent factor which horses appear to relish. A spoonful of molassine meal or even some honey will never go amiss and adds variety. Divide the ration into three feeds per day given slightly damp and as the work programme allows. In addition, give a good general supplement.

In these early days a soft meadow hay of the best quality, given in a small-mesh net, will be adequate. A coarser, more nutritious, seed hay can be mixed in with it towards the end of the primary training period.

Monitor the weight/feed ratio by taking regular measurements (once every two weeks is about right) and make adjustments to the feed on that basis.

Daily Routine

Before the horse is brought into work, plan the daily routine according to individual circumstances and once it has been successfully established stick to it.

The following is given as an example on the basis of the horse being stabled overnight and allowed a recreation period on the paddock in the middle of the day, but, clearly, it can be varied to fit in with the pertaining commitments and circumstance.

7.00 am	Quartering (brush-over, clean feet), pick up droppings, etc., 1st feed.
8.00 am	Muck out – grooming.
9.30 am	Exercise/work period.
10.30–11.00 am	Return to stables, groom, small hay net.
1.00 pm	2nd feed.
2–3.00 pm	Paddock recreation.
4.00 pm	Return to stable, hay net (say 1.8 kg/4 lb).
5–6.00 pm	Grooming, stable training.
7.00 pm	3rd feed.
9.00 pm	Last hay net (say 4.5 kg/10 lb).

However, it would not be advisable to get the young horse out of the paddock and begin the routine from Day 1. As with the feed intake it should be introduced by gradual stages over 7–14 days.

As a start, let the horse be walked quietly about the place giving him plenty of time to get used to the yard and its environs.

Take him into the box for a schooling period each day, letting him pick at a hay net while he is being handled. Maintain body contact with him and *talk* to him. In other words make friends with him and do make sure to handle him equally on *both* sides. It is just as important to avoid his becoming 'one-sided' in his mind as it is when he comes to be ridden.

Within the 7–14 days introductory period it should be possible to have the routine established, and within the next fortnight:

1. The horse should have been wormed.

2. The inoculation status should have been checked, brought up to date and entered on his documents.

3. Similarly, his mouth should have been inspected to establish the state of the teeth and anything untoward corrected.

4. He should have been checked over by a qualified physiotherapist for any signs of strain, soreness, etc.

Stable Lessons

Being Tied

One of the first lessons to teach the horse is to accept and submit to being tied. It is, indeed, a fundamental requirement on which much else depends. Horses are best tied up when being groomed or mucked out, for example. It is also advisable to tie them carefully when they are travelled and at some time it may be necessary to tie them to the trailer or horsebox when at a show or event.

As a safety measure it is often advocated that the horse be tied to a loop of string that will break easily should he run back. However, if he does go back and break the string he may very possibly acquire the habit of doing so, and that could become a major problem. (Very frequently, of course, the loop of string is a length of binder twine and that doesn't break nearly so easily.)

The horse can be taught to respect the restraint of the tie rope by making use of Galvayne's harness (as described in Part 2 – Additional Training Aids) or a variation of that piece of equipment, but it can be accomplished just as easily with an extra long rope passing from the headcollar, through the wall-ring and back to one's hand.

Almost invariably there will be some old horse-*breaker* who will talk about 'railway headcollars' and telegraph poles, but we are in the business of *making* young horses, not *breaking* them. (A 'railway headcollar' is a relic of the days when horses were routinely transported by rail. They were very heavy and strong enough to hold a rogue elephant. To this was attached a stout rope, which for good measure was possibly passed round the animal's head as well and then secured to a telegraph pole or some such immovable object. The horse was then left for some hours to get on with it, or he might be *encouraged* to run back until he learnt the impossibility of freeing himself. I know of other 'brute force and ignorance' methods, but they are all just as unnecessary and all are likely to be non-productive in terms of the end result.)

Holding the rope, as I suggest, it is still possible to handle and groom the horse lightly. If he moves back the rope is allowed to slip through the ring, then he can be encouraged to move forward and put in his original position again, while once more a light tension is taken up on the rope. Repeat the lesson a dozen times, saying 'No' on each occasion when he moves back and the horse will have learnt to stand still.

Otherwise, make yourself as comfortable as you can and hold the rope in the manner prescribed while feeding the horse from your hand. When, or if, he steps back encourage him to come forward again while saying 'Come here'. In that way he learns the tying lesson and a word of command, too. Thereafter, however, *always* tie the rope in a quick-release knot in case of emergencies.

Figure 33. Always, always secure the horse with a quick-release knot – just in case...

Box Manners

Although the box is the horse's home it is necessary for him to learn that he has to share his space when being attended to by his handler/trainer. For the sake of harmony and safety he has to understand that it is we who dictate his movements while we are in the box.

Blocking and Barging

A habit to be discouraged from Day 1 is that of blocking the doorway when one wishes to enter. It can be countered by placing a hand on the chest, saying 'Back' and giving a firm push so that he is in a position convenient to you. Should he not respond to the push on the chest, tread on his toes – it always works and it is better than having him tread on your toes.

Rather worse is the horse who barges for the door as soon as the headcollar or bridle is removed. With that in mind always position the horse in the same spot, away from the door, preparatory to removing his headgear and insist on his staying there, putting him firmly back into position if he moves.

Moving Over

He then needs to learn how to move from one side to another in response to a request from his handler.

This can be taught, initially, by holding the horse's head inclined towards your body and tapping his flank with a short stick or even the hand, while you give the command 'Move over' – another addition to the basic vocabulary. Inevitably the combination of head position and tap will result in the quarters being moved away or 'moved over'.

The next step is for the assistant to hold the horse's head in the same manner while the trainer stands just in advance of the hip and facing the front. From this position the tap and command are given as before. Gradually, it becomes possible to stand in line with the dock to give the command and indicate the required movement with the hand.

If an assistant is not available, the same result can be achieved by using the lead rope from the headcollar. In a surprisingly short time the rope will not be needed. The secret, of course, is in taking up the correct body position, which, in itself, tells the horse to which side he is being asked to move.

Later, when horse and helpers have got used to each other, one can move close up round the back of the horse and move him over with a click of the tongue and a pat from the appropriate hand. In these early days, however, it is best not to risk taking liberties with a young, inexperienced horse and to be definite and deliberate in your movements.

Grooming and Handling

The purpose of grooming is not just for the sake of appearance, but is a necessary practice in maintaining a healthy horse. Horses kept stabled for much of the day or night and fed on concentrated rations create a greater amount of waste matter. Much of it is dispersed through excrement and, when exercise/work increases the rate of breathing, waste carbon dioxide is expelled by the lungs. However, a significant quantity is dispersed through the skin pores and if that is to be accomplished it is necessary for the skin to be clean and the pores clear of dust, dried sweat, etc.

Grooming not only contributes materially to the health of the animal but it allows for a relationship to develop between horse and handler.

At the outset, grooming is no more than a light brush-over, but within a week or two it can be carried out with considerable vigour, the handler putting their full weight behind the brush strokes. After an energetic grooming session female handlers should *glow*, while men will have worked up a *sweat*.

Strapping

Strapping is an extension of grooming and is carried out even more energetically. Its purpose is to improve overall functional efficiency by stimulating circulation and promoting the growth and tonus of the muscular system. Normal grooming takes place after exercise, when the horse is warm and the skin pores are open. However, strapping is best left to the evening so as to encourage circulation which naturally slows down during the night hours.

The exercise needs, of course, to be approached by gradual stages and it is probably not advisable to think about it until one is between 4–6 weeks into the primary schooling – and even then it needs to be carried out at half-throttle for a week or so.

Strapping is often called '*wisping*' because it involves the employment of a dampened 'wisp' made from a tightly woven rope of hay. In fact, few people today would go to the trouble of making a conventional wisp, even if they knew how. (For the curious or the incurable traditionalist, a wisp is made by opening a hay bale, shaking it out a little and then twisting a rope of it while keeping the foot on the bulk of the bale. Two loops need then to be made at one end and the rope twisted between them. The end of the rope is secured by passing it through each loop and then tucking in the end securely. With a little practice and a couple of free afternoons the result should look a bit like the illustration – Figure 34.)

To use the wisp, first damp it and then bring it down energetically in rhythmical strokes following the lie of the coat. Use it on the quarters, shoulders and neck but *not on the loins, head, belly and legs*. Just as satisfactory for the purpose is a chamois leather stitched to make a small bag and then stuffed with hay until it is firm, otherwise many saddlers still supply a more sophisticated article in the form of a hay-stuffed leather pad.

Most horses enjoy being wisped and when a rhythm has been achieved the muscles contract and decontract visibly in time to the strokes of the wisp. It does wonders for the development of the muscles and produces a satisfying shine, or bloom, on the coat caused by the release of oil from the glands surrounding each hair.

A further massage technique can be employed by using the bare forearms after immersing them in a bucket of water. It is hard work but worthwhile and, in the modern climate, a wonderful 'bonding' exercise.

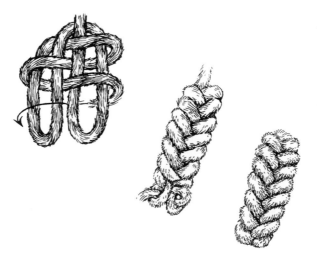

Figure 34. Hay wisp made from hay twisted into a rope. Used dampened it is very effective, moreover the making of it provides endless entertainment on a wet afternoon.

Focal Points of Handling

In the first weeks of the primary stage we should concentrate our efforts on three areas: the feet, the head and the mouth.

A properly brought up young horse will already have been accustomed to having his *feet* handled, and will probably have had them dressed by the farrier. But take nothing for granted, especially if the horse is not home-bred.

Make a point of picking up the feet and cleaning them out whenever you are in the box. Use the word 'Lift', or any other word you fancy, as you get your hand on the leg. If you persist it is quite possible to teach the horse to raise the foot on the word of command.

From the outset young horses should be accustomed to having their feet handled as matter of course.

Have the farrier call to trim the feet as soon as you are sure that the horse will be entirely co-operative. It is no bad idea, indeed, to let the youngster watch an older horse being shod and let him learn from the good example set by his more mature companion. At about week 6 it is advisable to have the young horse shod but again take the precaution of having the older horse present.

With a competent farrier there should be no problem, but it is possible that the horse's action may be affected by a very little for a day or two while the youngster becomes used to the feel of the shoes.

Head-shy horses are exasperating and so time spent talking to the young horse while stroking his neck and rubbing his ears is never wasted.

Handling the *mouth* is just as important. Essentially, the mouth should be looked at as part of the daily routine and always after the horse has been ridden. Young horses go through a continual process of shedding milk teeth and replacing them with permanent ones up to the age of six, when they are said to have a 'full mouth'. Frequently, during the process, the gums will

Nothing is more exasperating than the head-shy horse. Make a point of handling the ears very frequently.

Handling the mouth is all part of the young horse's education. It should be examined routinely on a daily basis.

become inflamed and like a child in the same situation the horse may be fractious and irritable. We can help by rubbing the affected area with tincture of myrrh or even a little whisky and knowing the problem we can make allowances for minor lapses in behaviour; but, of course, we can hardly appreciate what is amiss unless we have carried out a daily inspection of the mouth.

To open the mouth it is only necessary to insert finger and thumb *gently* behind the lower jaw while saying 'Open wide' or something similar. Since the fingers are over the bars of the mouth between molars and incisors there is no chance of being bitten.

Fitting the Bit

Fitting the bit should present no problems if the mouth is handled on a regular basis. Nonetheless, it is as well to take a few elementary precautions. First, remove the browband, so that the ears do not have to be pulled through, and unfasten the nearside cheek from the headpiece. Slip the headpiece over the poll, open the mouth and with the left hand take the bit over the lower jaw. A slice of carrot laid over the bit is a useful encouragement and once the latter is in the mouth the nearside cheekpiece can be fastened. (Before starting this little exercise make sure that the cheekpieces are adjusted equally and at a proper length. A hole too long can be remedied when the bit is in the mouth, but take care that the cheeks are not too short and pull the bit upwards against the corners of the mouth.)

The bridle can remain in place for a few minutes each time it is fitted to give the horse time to 'mouth' the bit. Once the horse has accepted the bit the bridle can be put on in the usual way, but when a browband is fitted use one a couple of sizes too big so as to avoid struggling with the ears. There is, however, no need for a browband when the bridle is worn under the lunge cavesson. In this circumstance the bridle is fitted just to get the horse used to its feel in the mouth.

Exercise and Work

There is a difference between these two terms. Exercise is given at slow speeds over an extended period and is relatively undemanding. Work is demanding of greater energy and concentration; it occupies a shorter space of time and is interspersed with frequent periods of rest.

Introduction to Lungeing Equipment and Practices

In the early primary schooling the concern is largely with exercise as an introduction to work on the lunge.

From the outset the horse wears his lunge cavesson with the stud-fastening browband in place. Both nose-piece and jowl strap need to fit snugly. The lunge rein is fitted to the centre ring of the cavesson, the rein being held some 75 cm (30 in) down its length and the remainder passed across the trainer's body, where it can be held neatly looped in the outside hand.

The long, training whip is held in the outside hand, point downwards, and from the beginning the horse is led equally from *both* sides to discourage any inclination towards a permanent bend round the trainer. The ideal is for the trainer to be positioned at the horse's shoulder, the horse walking out slightly in advance.

As a start the assistant, carrying a lunge whip, follows up behind so that she can urge the horse forward if necessary. To do so it will only be necessary to have the horse aware of the whip's presence.

The horse has also to learn about the trainer's whip and to respect it. To start the lesson it is useful to place the horse alongside a wall or railings to prevent his swinging the quarters outwards. A tweak on the lunge line will obtain his attention and when he is standing square the command 'Walk-March' is given, quite sharply, while the whip taps his flank behind the trainer's back.

In the walk we want the horse to stride out boldly and freely to his front, while the hand allows him to stretch forward without imposing any restriction on the nose and certainly not twisting the head inwards. Indeed, the hand, whether it holds a lunge line or a bridle rein, acts in just the same way. It follows the movement of the horse's head, maintaining a contact and restraining when necessary by intermittent tensions applied by the fingers.

Walking In-hand

Walking in-hand is a most important exercise, although its value is not always sufficiently recognized. It teaches obedience to the voice and respect for the whip, both of which are lessons in submission, a word that may not find favour with the touchy-feely school, though submission is integral to the human-equine relationship which has safe, enjoyable riding as its objective. Moreover, it sets the foundations for free, *forward* movement, the second of General L'Hotte's commandments.

The walk in-hand. The horse strides boldly forward without restriction and certainly without the head being pulled to the inside.

The horse has also to learn to halt on command, a matter that involves the use of body, hand, whip and *voice*.

To halt the horse, the trainer lengthens stride to be in advance of the horse's shoulder, then turns inwards towards the horse, acting with the rein hand to check him, and then brings up the butt-end of the whip in front of the horse's nose. Simultaneously, the command 'Whoa' is given in a long, drawn out tone. The horse is then asked to stand up square and is rewarded for his co-operation. It is important, even at this early stage, to get him to stand square. If he is allowed to get into the habit of halting unevenly with a trailing hind leg it will persist under saddle, when it is far more difficult to correct.

If the horse does not come squarely to halt he is in no position to move off smartly into walk, much less into trot or canter or, indeed, to rein-back when we come to teaching that movement. He is, in short, unbalanced and must first bring up his trailing hind leg before taking a step forward.

However, because he is yet not fully developed the horse may experience difficulty in making a square halt. He can be helped if the halt is asked for on a shallow curve. If, for instance, he trails the left hind leg a curve left will cause that leg to be engaged further under the body and if the request to halt is correctly timed it will probably stay there.

There is no reason why we should not introduce the trot from walk for short periods. The same principles apply but it must be kept slow yet active and the transition from trot to walk must be as smooth as we can get it. The word of command in this instance is 'Terrot' with the accent on the last syllable.

The trot in-hand, free, active and in a very good outline. While the leader should never be in advance of the shoulder she must take care not to be too far behind it. Young horses are well able to deliver a crafty cow-kick.

Somewhere between weeks 4–6 we should have effected a painless introduction to the simple lunge exercises, from which point we teach the 'three Rs' which will culminate in the horse being backed and ridden.

Before that, however, it will be as well to remind ourselves of the objectives implicit in the lunge exercises.

Lungeing

The lunge exercises are fundamental to the training of the young horse, but to be beneficial they must be carried out correctly. Conversely, inexpert lungeing can do real damage to the structure and the freedom of the gaits.

The objectives of lungeing are both *physical* and *mental*.

The *physical objectives* are:

1. The promotion of muscular development *without it being formed in opposition to the rider's weight*. Additionally, and importantly, the equal development of muscles on *either* side of the body.

2. The suppling of the horse laterally by the equal stretching and contraction of the dorsal, neck and abdominal muscles on each side.

3. The induction of a degree of tension (tone) in the spinal complex by encouraging extension and a lowering of the head and neck in response to the increased engagement of the hind legs. On the circle the inside hind leg is bound to be more actively engaged beneath the body than its partner.

4. The increase in the flexion of the joints as a result of greater and more supple muscular development.

5. The correction of any natural curvature of the body that causes the hind legs to be carried away from the track of the forelegs. A natural curvature is apparent as the foal lies in the womb and it is frequently compounded by handling and leading the horse from the nearside while neglecting the offside. In most instances mature horses show greater development along the right-hand side of the body, which is one reason why horses work more easily to the left than the right. For this reason it is important to work the horse on both the left and right rein, probably giving greater prominence to the latter.

6. The improvement of the balance arising from greater engagement of the quarters and the refinement of the gaits, particularly in terms of rhythm, which may be defined as 'the regularity and correctly ordered flow of the gait', and tempo – the rate of the stride or footfall.

Mentally, the lunge work:

1. Encourages the maintenance of a state of *calm*.

2. Teaches the acceptance and development of habitual discipline and, in particular, obedience to the *voice*.

3. Is a powerful tool in the development of *forward movement*, which is as much a mental as a physical quality.

Method

The lunge work is a natural extension of the work in-hand and is taught from that base. It begins with the trainer lengthening the rein, stepping back a pace or two so that the body is in line with the horse's hip, and letting the horse walk round in a circle.

Thereafter, the assistant can lead the horse round the trainer, using a lead rein fastened to the *outside* ring of the cavesson. Usually, it is recommended that the assistant leads from the inside of the circle. I prefer her to lead from the opposite side so that her body is not positioned between me and the horse. She does not then come between us and the horse is better able to concentrate on me and I on him. I do not belong to the touchy-feely, psycho-babble school but I understand that in communicating with the horse I have to use the power of my mind as well as my body-language and the supporting aids of the whip and the lunge rein.

The assistant is also of enormous help in getting the horse to understand and obey the voice, reinforcing, if necessary, the trainer's words of command. While the trainer makes much use of the voice, the vocal commands have to be underlined with the rein and the whip.

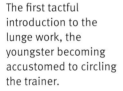

The first tactful introduction to the lunge work, the youngster becoming accustomed to circling the trainer.

Transitions

In the downward transitions from trot to walk to halt, the command is drawn out and possibly prefaced by a 'Steady, boy, steady', accompanied by a tensioning of the rein made with little jerks of the fingers. As the horse responds, the command 'Waalk, waalk' is given, the rein tension ceasing as the horse takes up that gait. In fact, it is not easy for a young horse to return to walk from trot smoothly and he relies on getting some help from his trainer. Conversely, it is not easy for the trainer to obtain smooth transitions. It is a skill acquired by practice and a good deal of concentration.

For halt, 'Whoa' is the most convenient choice simply because it is easier to draw the word out. Having obtained the halt one can go out to the horse, stand him up square and then pat him in reward, or even let him have a small titbit.

To obtain the upward transitions use of the whip is made in a brushing movement along the ground, again to emphasize the vocal command. The rein is held with sufficient tension to keep the horse to the circle but one has to be careful that it does not interrupt the movement.

Exemplary downward stretching at walk showing engagement of the hind legs and a well-rounded outline.

Changing the Rein

There are those who bring the horse in towards the centre as a preparation for changing the rein. I prefer to halt the horse, walk out to him, change over my whip and rein and move myself to the opposite side before asking him to go on and taking up my position in line with his hip. I do so because I do not want to encourage the horse to turn in at any time. Of course, that will not happen while the assistant is using the lead rein but within two or three lessons she should be able to move further away, finally relinquishing the lead rein and taking up a position a few yards behind the horse, from which she can urge him forward if necessary.

Circle Size

Once the trainer is lungeing the horse unaccompanied, work can begin towards more accurate circles and an altogether more active movement can be asked for at trot, which is the most beneficial of the gaits on the lunge. Nonetheless, the circles must be kept large. Too small a circle is restrictive of the movement and causes the quarters to be carried outside the track. It is essential that the trainer moves with the horse in concentric circles and at all times is conscious of maintaining the *triangle of control*. To do so the trainer, standing in a line just behind the horse's hip, represents the apex of the triangle, while the whip and the rein form the two sides. Always the horse goes forward from the whip into the hand, just as later he will go forward into the bit from the action of the rider's legs.

Resistance and Evasion

Not unnaturally there will be occasional resistances, and they have to be met quickly and with resolution. I will not say that 'He has to know who's boss' – that would be too redolent of force – but he does need to be reminded unequivocally of the rules of the game.

Sometimes, the horse may attempt to turn about, particularly when working in the direction that he finds more difficult. Usually, he will turn inwards and it is then that we must move swiftly to get behind him, sending him forwards with energetic movements of the whip *without ever hitting him*.

Of course, he may simply attempt to take off. In that situation there is really no point in entering into a trial of strength with a half-ton horse intent on getting loose. Instead, we must go with him as best we can, restraining him with a series of sharp tugs on the rein, while speaking to him in a quiet tone of voice. In the end we will regain control, for the cavesson is a powerful instrument. It is for that reason that while we remain resolute in our efforts to obtain control we must be careful not to injure the horse. Probably, it is possible to stop a young horse by force but we risk his being spun round on the forelegs and sustaining damage in the way of strains and sprains.

Occasionally, a fresh young horse will disregard the request to halt, which need not worry us too much. Usually a flip on the rein, causing a ripple down its length that ends with a smack on his nose will be sufficient. Should he persist he will certainly stop if he is driven into the wall of the *manège*, but we should reserve that form of correction as a last resort.

Two difficulties arise from working on the circle. In the first instance the horse may continually fall in toward the centre; in the second he pulls against the rein. The former is a way of avoiding the effort entailed in bending on the circle and is combated by pointing or flicking the whip at the horse's shoulder. Pulling against the rein is the horse's way of telling you that the circle is too tight for comfort. The solution is to make it larger and thus remove the cause of his difficulty.

Less frequent, but by no means unknown, is the horse who comes into the centre in an attempt to intimidate and test the authority of the trainer. A swift sideways move to get behind him and send him forward again will usually work. Otherwise, one has to counter-attack, moving forward res- olutely to show him that far from being frightened one is determined to retaliate strongly. Thereafter, five minutes going somewhat faster than is comfortable for him will ensure that the message gets home.

Most young horses, and certainly the best ones, will try at some point in their training to pick a fight (resist deliberately) in an attempt to test the trainer's authority. Young children do the same thing and in the case of the horse it is best that he gets it out of his system sooner rather than later.

Occasionally there will be moments of resistance made as much from high spirits as otherwise. Note the horse is wearing roller and crupper.

Now wearing the side-reins the young horse decides to assert himself, but his trainer is not impressed.

Roller and Crupper

When the horse has become used to the introductory lunge exercises it is time to work towards obtaining improved carriage, balance and gaits. All will be more easily attained by the careful use of side-reins, which will also, in later stages, accustom him to making contact with the bit. Side-reins, however, require a point of anchorage, which is supplied by a body roller, and the horse needs to become accustomed to working with the roller in place. To complete the lunge tackle there is the crupper, which may as well be fitted at this point as any other.

The horse who has been well handled is likely to accept the roller without trouble, but it is as well to get him used to it by gradual stages. As a start, put it in his manger or wherever convenient while he is being groomed, allowing him to sniff at it and touch it with his nose. This is the theory, but in reality he is unlikely to make more than a token acknowledgement of its presence. Nor is he likely to make any objection when a soft pad is placed over his back, followed by the roller itself. He might just evince a little apprehension when the roller is fastened round his middle, but he will, of course, have been used to the fastenings of a rug. Put it on and off half-a-dozen times in the course of a day or two and during that time fit the crupper (see Lungeing Equipment in Part 2.) Leave the tackle in place for an hour or two at a time and lead the horse round the box with it in place.

When he is first lunged in the roller, which will then need to be adjusted to fit snugly, the horse may be a little reluctant to go forward initially and may even indulge in a half-hearted buck. Take no notice – he will soon settle.

Here we see a confident, free trot, the young horse engaging his hind legs and showing an acceptable outline.

Poles and Grids

'Give me some poles and I'll make you a horse.'

With the horse working at trot in acceptable circles, carrying head and neck naturally and fairly low but with noticeable engagement of the quarters, it is time to introduce the invaluable ground-pole exercises.

The use of ground-poles encourage an improved rhythm, greater hock engagement and a noticeable stretching of head and neck forwards and downwards, actions which contribute to the improvement of the top-line.

Otherwise pole work acts as a strengthening and suppling exercise, while contributing to the rounding of the form and is, importantly, the first introduction to jumping.

Begin with one stout pole laid on the long side of the arena. The horse is first led over the pole at walk and then at trot on both reins without any

Working over ground poles. In this instance the poles are set on an element of a circle. It is a difficult exercise and demands a high level of skill on the part of the trainer.

attempt being allowed to rush or jump the pole. *Don't work at trot until the exercise is well-established at walk.*

Within the space of two lessons add a further pole on the other side of the arena; follow that with a grid of three poles and then with a five-pole grid. The grid work is a trot exercise and the distance between the poles is crucial. For most horses 1.45–1.5 m (4 ft 10in–5 ft) will be convenient, but adjustments are necessary for a long-striding horse or, conversely, for one with a significantly shorter stride.

As the horse becomes more proficient in the exercise the poles can be raised from the ground on low blocks and in the later stages the height can be increased to 50 cm (20 in).

To work over the grid of poles it is, of course, necessary for the approach to be made on a straight line with the trainer working close to the horse. In the more advanced exercises the grid can be placed on the circle, which is altogether more demanding.

At this point, say 3–4 weeks into the programme, the side-reins are best fitted, initially, to the rings of the cavesson, being transferred to the bit rings within two or three lessons. Used in the manner described in Part 2 – Lungeing Equipment they contribute materially to the making of the mouth and, of course, to the overall carriage.

The young horse jumping confidently on the lunge.

below A jump being made in excellent outline. Clearly, the horse is enjoying himself.

A horse being lunged in the saddle. The walk is entirely relaxed and is being used as a 'rest' gait. All lungeing sessions should start and finish with a period of walk.

Notes on the Lunge Exercises

While the trot is the main gait of the lunge and the most rewarding in terms of development, outline and rhythm, the walk must not be neglected.

While the trot represents work, the walk is the introductory gait in which, and from which, one consolidates obedience to the commands and begins the variations within the gaits.

It can be a gait of rest, but we need also to work on its freedom, activity and rhythm. In any event, every lunge exercise and every ridden lesson should begin and end with a period of walk.

The gait employs a great many muscles without their being under extreme exertion. As a result the muscles remain more or less flat, sliding easily and smoothly over each other with a gentle pulsating action. It is a preparation for the more strenuous trot work, easing any stiffness and acting towards an increase in circulation.

Without this preparatory loosening preceding the trot work there is the danger of the muscle fibres becoming bunched and causing the movement to be stiffened and restricted commensurately.

After work the gentler action of the walk helps the muscles get rid of waste products which will have accumulated under stress (the word being used advisedly in the physical sense). It also helps smooth out muscle fibres which may have become taut or even 'knotted'.

When work in trot commences, the aim is to obtain a good working gait, head and neck stretched down, hind legs engaged and top-line nicely rounded; *the latter will, therefore, be long while the bottom line will be short.*

If it is the opposite of that desirable state you have an upside-down horse, on the forehand and hopelessly out of balance.

Obtain the outline by pushing forward through the agency of the whip into contact with the rein, then ask for the stretch by alternately tightening and relaxing the hand.

By week 3–4 it should be possible to obtain a few lengthened steps in trot and also to vary the size of the circles, decreasing the radius for a few circuits and then enlarging it. The practice, which will certainly not be perfected until we are a little way into the secondary, four-year-old schooling, is invaluable in improving the balance and the carriage. Larger circles contribute to lengthening, while smaller ones act conversely.

Lengthening of the stride is brought about by pushing the horse forward into a hand that resists momentarily to prevent the pace from just becoming faster. The increased engagement of the hind legs under those circumstances produces a commensurate lengthening in the stride taken by the forelegs.

Check Points

Watch continually for the correct tracking up of the hind feet.

When working in side-reins from the bit, the mouth should be closed while the lips have a covering of white foam (the classic soapy mouth).

The ears should be relaxed and the tail carried freely, swinging loosely from the quarters. If it is clamped down and tucked inwards the back will be stiff and hard.

If the ears are carried one up and one down, the head is being twisted at the poll in resistance. It is a sure sign of over-tight side-reins.

The abdominal muscles provide a reliable indication of relaxation or otherwise. If they are noticeably held up tightly we have a tense horse, a matter reflected in the freedom of the gait. However, there will always be a tensioning of the muscles of the abdomen – a degree of tonicity – when the muscles of the top-line are stretched to produce a rounded outline.

To obtain the ideal relaxation may take up to ten minutes or more and so it cannot be expected until, at the end of the 3–4 week period, we are able to extend the work period up to thirty minutes or so.

Flexions, Long-Reining and Transitions In-Hand

Introducing the horse to the action of the bit, and work on long-reins, can begin in the week 3–6 period.

Bit Flexions

It seems logical that the young horse should be accustomed to the action of the bit before he is actually backed and ridden from the mouth.

In times past much was made of the 'flexions' and they were practised assiduously. The word and the practice is now outdated but then very little is heard about 'making a mouth' today and there is certainly less evidence of 'made mouths'.

Although the flexions involved with the double bridle (introduced in the four-year-old secondary phase of training) are naturally more complex, those practised with the snaffle are simple enough and initially they take up no more than the odd five minutes when the horse is in his stable.

They are carried out with the horse positioned with his tail to the wall to dissuade him from moving backwards.

Standing at the shoulder, facing the front, the trainer takes both reins, one in each hand, holding them about 30 cm (1 ft) behind the mouth and the distance of the bit apart. The fingers then vibrate the reins gently to induce the horse to drop his nose and relax the lower jaw. The reins can then be vibrated separately to obtain a similar relaxation on *each side* of the mouth. When a single rein is operated its partner must, of course, allow for the action by ceding very slightly to the front.

Should the young horse attempt to evade the action by stepping back it is probably because the hand is acting too strongly, otherwise the presence of the assistant to pat his rear-end (without standing directly behind him) will solve the problem.

These elementary flexions can be taken a stage further in the school just before finishing the work for the day. With the trainer taking a position at the shoulder the horse is persuaded with the help of the assistant to walk forward. When the command 'Whoa' is given the reins are vibrated as before. In fact in this instance the reins are best applied alternately, rather than simultaneously, so that the horse is never given a fixed base against which to resist; the pressure shifting smoothly from one side to the other.

The directional changes are taught by the vibration of a single rein accompanied by a shift of the hand outwards, causing the horse to make a shallow turn.

The exercises need take no more than a few minutes and when the horse responds he should, naturally, be rewarded before returning to his stable.

Long-Reining

To take the mouthing process a stage further we can have recourse to the long-reins. Long-reining does require a degree of skill and dexterity but it is less difficult than might be supposed. One skilled exponent of the art likened it to wallpapering a room, a daunting task for many householders. 'Once one is brave enough to make a start', he opined, 'it just gets easier as you go along.'

Long-reining teaches obedience to the indications of the rein while at the same time it encourages an improvement in balance, carriage and the quality of the gaits – all achieved without the inhibiting weight of the rider on the horse's back.

Very skilled exponents, like the late Einar Schmit Jensen and his gifted pupil Sylvia Stanier, who gave memorable displays at London's Horse of the Year Show, produced the most advanced movements, including passage and piaffe, for example, but even lesser mortals can make significant improvements in the horse's outline, action and responses. (All of us, of course, will benefit from reading Miss Stanier's book *The Art of Long Reining*, published by J. A. Allen. *Long Reining – The Saumur Method* by Philippe Karl, also published by J.A. Allen is another book that is well worth studying.)

Figure 35. Long-reining in the French method, the horse being driven forward from behind the quarters.

A further and very important benefit to be derived from long-rein driving is in building free forward movement while adding immeasurably to the horse's confidence. The young horse can be driven round the yard and on bridleways and quiet lanes (if there are any left) and also in open country where, so long as the handler is sufficiently agile, he can negotiate small banks and ditches and even pop over low obstacles like a conveniently sited log.

There are various long-reining techniques and some differences in the equipment made. They range from those based on the practices of the classical schools to the less sophisticated and correspondingly more limited methods practised by British and Irish horsemen. Nonetheless, the latter can produce excellent results in the training of the young horse, particularly, in my view, when a roller of the sort described in Part 2 – Saddlery and Equipment is used rather than when the reins are passed through the stirrup irons of a saddle, an arrangement favoured by some trainers.

The long-rein exercise assists in the mouthing process and encourages an improvement in balance, carriage and the quality of the gaits. However, it might be considered 'over the top' to go to the trouble of plaiting the mane for the exercise.

General Method of Long-reining

Initially, the horse is driven from the cavesson rings, not from the bit. The lunge line, to which the horse is well-accustomed, is moved to the inside of the three cavesson rings, while the second rein is attached to the outer one and then passed via the top ring on the roller, round the quarters and back to the hand.

The horse is then lunged in the usual fashion and given time to get used to the rein round his quarters. Should he object strongly, the outside rein can be dropped in an emergency, while control is maintained through the inside lunge rein.

When the horse accepts the situation, the assistant can lead him while the trainer operates the reins, both of which can then be passed through the roller rings.

In a short time the horse will circle quite confidently on his own, so long as the trainer is positioned three-quarters on to his rear and remains within his vision. He can, however, become worried when the trainer takes up a driving position directly behind him and is almost out of sight. It is then that he is likely to become hesitant and lose confidence and will need the reassurance of the trainer's voice.

Working on large circles it is not difficult to change the rein by getting the horse to pass in front of you and then for you to move quietly to the opposite side.

Bit and Side-reins

Once good forward movement is established the reins can be transferred to the bit and the side-reins fitted loose enough to hang in a shallow loop. The work can then proceed at both walk and trot with changes of direction, 'slow-downs and speed-ups', with the stride being shortened and lengthened, being practised for short periods within those gaits. It is, however, essential to avoid work on tight circles which inhibit both gait and forward movement and may also cause physical damage.

Use of the Hands

Obviously, a sympathetic, light use of the reins is an essential factor, the necessity for which is emphasized by the length (and weight) of rein between hand and mouth. The hands need always to keep a light, unbroken contact and to that end must be ready to take up any slackness that occurs. *Never*, however, must they descend to pulling.

The principles to be observed are that the inside rein produces flexion and the outer, by supporting, contributes to the balance.

Ideally, the reins are worked in time to the movement of the hind legs, but it is easier, I think, for the less expert to watch the forelegs, taking the rein a little to maintain the rhythm as the corresponding foreleg is raised, i.e. left rein with left foreleg and vice versa.

In making changes of direction we should comply with the logical classical precept of giving with the *outside* rein instead of *pulling* with the inside one.

The worst failing in the British instructional system – one that nonetheless, and possibly remarkably, produces more practical, all-round horsemen and women per capita than any other – was the emphasis given to 'feeling' the inside rein to make a directional change. Unfortunately it was more often than not interpreted in the mind of the novice rider (and teacher) as, 'Pull with the left to go left, pull with the right to go right', a practice that inevitably resulted in interrupting and restricting the stride pattern as well as resulting in a loss of balance and, of course, of forward movement. What is meant by riding on the outside rein is that, in making a turn, the inside hand, carried outwards a little to emphasize the direction of the movement, maintains its light contact, while that on the outside of the mouth is eased by the hand moving forward to allow the bend in the required direction. No shortening of the stride or disruption in the gait is then possible.

Driving off the Circle

A most important part of the long-rein work is when the horse is driven forward from directly behind his quarters. This allows the trainer to put the horse into an even more positive contact with the bit and to encourage a greater degree of self-carriage. Of course, it is best performed along an enclosing fence or wall that helps in keeping the horse straight.

Transitions and Rein-Back in-Hand

Towards the end of the primary schooling we should be able to consolidate the transitions upward from halt to trot and the other way about, and also to introduce the rein-back.

This last movement can become something of a *bête noir* to the novice rider (as well as to the more advanced ones), probably because it is attempted too early in the ridden training without the horse having been sufficiently prepared, a matter that may also be applied to the rider.

It is obtained from halt and is made easier if the assistant lends a helping hand, or foot. The horse is driven forward energetically into a *square* halt, a ragged, one-leg trailing stop is not sufficient and will be wholly non-productive, since the posture has first to be corrected *before* the horse can step back in two-time, i.e. diagonal legs moving simultaneously.

With the poll and lower jaw flexed and relaxed the movement is obtained by asking the horse to move *forward*. Just as he begins to obey, the hands close on the reins intermittently with the usual vibration of the fingers. If the assistant stands at his front and taps his chest it helps the horse to understand what is wanted of him. Two or three distinct steps to the rear are quite enough and the horse should be sent forward again. (It is possible, and is often advocated, to apply the reins alternately. It is effective when practised by an experienced trainer but if one has doubts on that score is best left alone for the time being.)

Under saddle, the rein-back is usually asked for late in the training of the four-year-old when the horse is more experienced. However, there is no harm in laying foundations for the movement at this stage.

Backing

At some point in the first half of the primary training (during weeks 6–8 approximately) the horse is made accustomed to the saddle on his back. The sequence leading to his being mounted by a rider is this:

1. In the stable, the saddle is put on the horse's back when, for the most part, he is likely to accept it without demur, being already accustomed to his roller.

2. He learns to work in the saddle and to accept the presence of the stirrups.

3. A rider is put on his back and the horse, having accepted the weight, begins to learn how to carry it.

Introducing the Saddle

The saddle is best introduced after work when the horse will have got the itch out of his heels. Once more, it does no harm to put the saddle in the manger or wherever for a few days before putting it on the horse's back. He may touch it with his nose but it is just as likely that he will ignore it entirely.

Put the saddle on quietly over a well-fitting numnah with the girth fastened on the offside and passed over the top of the seat, the irons run up the leathers and secured as shown in Figure 36.

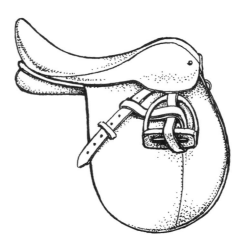

Figure 36.
A recommended method of securing the irons when the horse is lunged with the saddle in place.

Quietly does it. In a quiet corner of the school the rider lies across the horse's back.

The assistant can then move round the horse to pass the girth under his belly to the trainer standing on the nearside, and it can be fastened gradually, to a reasonable degree of tightness. The procedure can be carried out for a few days, while the assistant can lean over the saddle from either side to accustom the horse to weight over his back. So long as the young horse has been prepared adequately and well handled it is unlikely that he will be worried, but he might be more concerned when he is first led out and lunged with the saddle in place.

He will wear his cavesson over the bridle with the side-reins fitted to the bit and attached to the first girth strap on either side, and will be led for a few circuits round the arena. Thereafter he is worked on the lunge in the normal fashion, though he may indulge in the odd bucking fit as he gets used to the creak of the leather and the movement of the flaps. However, *do ensure that the girth is sufficiently tight*, it would never do were the saddle to slip round.

Within a day or two the irons can be let down the leathers, but take the precaution of tying them together under the belly with a piece of binder twine to prevent their swinging about unduly.

Introducing the Rider

The next step is to put the rider up, a proceeding best carried out at the end of the work session. For a day or two it is enough if the assistant, wearing a hard hat of course, lies over the saddle and the horse, having been led forward for a couple of strides is rewarded before she slips off.

Then comes the moment of truth – although, in fact, it is usually quite free of any dramatic element. After working, take the horse into a corner of the arena, remove the irons and let the assistant, making use of either a

The rider in place and the horse accepting the situation.

straw bale or a quick leg-up, first lie across the horse and then, keeping the body low, slip a leg over the horse's back, taking care not to kick the horse while doing so. Meantime, the horse can be distracted by much petting and a bowl of titbits, while the assistant moves her legs forward and back, a new experience for the horse but one he has to learn to accept.

Within a week, or probably less, the horse can be led round the arena with the rider in place and assuming an upright posture. At this juncture a rein to the hand replaces the side-reins and it is sensible to fit a neckstrap in case of emergencies.

Thereafter, the rider can use stirrups while the horse is worked on the lunge, round the arena in both directions, the line being attached to the cavesson as usual.

Early days. The horse being ridden quietly under the supervision of the trainer.

Communication

First Steps – Transitions

Initially, control is with the trainer, the horse obeying the vocal commands reinforced by appropriate body positioning and the action of the whip. Gradually, control passes to the rider through the latter's hands, legs and body-weight – although to be successful much depends on the rider using those aids clearly and consistently.

To teach *walk from halt* the rider first takes up the reins, while momentarily increasing the contact with the horse through the legs. Thereafter:

1. Rider applies legs in a positive, forward-rolling squeeze while opening fingers to remove tension on the rein. (In simple terms, pressing the accelerator and releasing the handbrake to allow a forward movement.)

2. Almost simultaneously, the trainer gives the command 'Walk-on' supported by a movement of the whip along the ground behind the horse.

3. In response to the horse moving forward, the leg, while being held in light contact ceases to act (fulfilling the principle of the aids – Prepare – Act – Yield). The hand, meanwhile, maintains light contact and follows the movement of the head.

The young horse going forward calmly and in a very acceptable outline.

To halt from walk:

1. The rider acts momentarily with the legs to push forward, while closing the fingers in intermittent squeezes and inclining the shoulders a little to the rear.

2. To reinforce the rider's aids the trainer gives the command 'Whoa' and puts a little tension on the lunge line.

To trot from walk:

1. The legs are applied in intermittent forward-rolling squeezes, the fingers being opened to allow for the increase in pace.

2. The trainer reinforces the aids through the medium of voice and whip.

At this stage the rider *rises* to the trot; the horse is not yet ready to carry the rider's weight in sitting trot.

As the work proceeds the trainer can take up an increasingly secondary role, dispensing with the lunge line and allowing control to pass wholly to the rider, who will then be able to make use of the full arena.

Working at trot the gait is active, the outline acceptable and there is a notable stillness in the mouth.

Changes of Direction

Using the full school area, changing the rein across the diagonal and riding large circles and loops involves the horse learning the turning or directional aids. Carried out correctly the circles, including the negotiation of corners, which in themselves are elements of the circle, as well as the simple directional changes, including loops and basic serpentines, lay the foundations for more advanced movements.

Together with the transitions and the elementary shortening and lengthening of the stride within the individual gaits they constitute the '3 Rs' in the schooling of the balanced, obedient and comfortable riding horse.

We make a directional change on the arc of a circle when we ride round each corner of the school. To turn the corner in balance and without loss of impulsion the rider must apply the aids consistently and with absolute clarity, thinking always of 'bending' the horse round the inside leg (even though that is not physically possible) and regarding the turn not as a distinct left or right movement but as an element of a circle.

Entering the corner with a good bend and notable engagement of the hind leg.

In fact, to ride a full circuit of the manège involves the execution of four quarter voltes, one at each corner of the arena. (A volte is a small circle of determined size, a circle proper being of any sizes larger than that. Theoretically, the radius of the volte is equal to the length of the horse, that is, on average, around 3 m (10 ft), the diameter being 6 m (20 ft).

To perform so small a circle is *very* difficult and beyond the capability of horses in the secondary, four-year-old, stage of schooling, who will certainly be compelled to swing his quarters outwards. (Just as frequently it is beyond the capacity of the rider, too.)

As an exercise in the possible, it is better to make the corners rounder. The bend can be the equivalent of a much larger circle of say 15 m (50 ft), when the horse's hind legs should be able to follow the track of the forefeet.

To ride the corners calls for:

1. Increased use of the legs on the approach combined with a slightly firmer rein contact but *no increase in speed.*

2. A stronger use of the inside leg as the curve is begun, together with a weighting of the inside iron (accomplished by the foot pushing downwards). The outside leg supports by being laid flat behind the girth.

3. The inside rein to be carried outwards (the *opening* rein) while the outside rein allows for the bend by the advance of the outside hand, elbow, shoulder *and* the outside hip.

The philosophy is that of riding from the inside leg to the outside hand and necessitates the rejection of some pretty sacred cows. It should be noted that at no time is the rider encouraged to *act* with the *outside* rein. For the most part the practice of that mistaken instruction results in a strong feel being taken of the *inside* rein against the base provided by the so-called supporting rein. In consequence the movement is impeded and shortened quite hopelessly.

Changes of Stride Length and Outline

To shorten and lengthen the stride is to contribute to the longitudinal suppling of the horse and the greater engagement of the quarters. It is, indeed, a very elementary exercise in improving balance. It is best at this stage to ride a few strides on the short side of the arena in shorter outline and then extend the stride down the long sides. It is accomplished by:

1. The more active employment of the legs, the driving aids, sending the horse forward into intermittently resisting hands so as to effect a shortening of the horse's base.

2. Lengthening is accomplished by opening the fingers.

Changing the Diagonal

From the outset the rider should be meticulous about 'changing the diagonal' at trot when changing the rein (i.e. when changing from circling right to circling left and vice versa.)

It is usual at rising trot on the left rein for the rider's seat to touch down on the saddle as the left foreleg and right hind leg come down on the circle left (the *inside* diagonal) while the opposite is the case when the circle, or the element of the circle, is to the right.

The seat rises from the saddle on the *outside* diagonal as the right shoulder moves forward on the circle left.

To change the diagonal the rider sits for one stride, before rising on the opposite diagonal. A quick downward glance at the appropriate shoulder will confirm which diagonal is being used, i.e. right shoulder forward on outside diagonal for circle left and vice versa.

It is argued, with every justification, that the rider's *inside* leg is applied more effectively and more easily when sitting in the saddle than when the seat is raised. The application of the *inside* leg, the operative one, when riding the circles and making directional changes, activates the increased engagement of the horse's corresponding hind leg beneath the body.

In addition to this, changing the diagonal is of even more importance to the horse's muscular development and movement. Should the rider always sit on the same diagonal, the horse's back muscles develop accordingly to cope with the situation. In short, the muscles on one side are developed more than those on the other and this certainly contributes to the horse becoming 'one-sided'.

(The walk is a gait of four separate beats made by the successive placing of each lateral pair of feet. The sequence when the walk begins on the left hind leg is: left hind, left fore, right hind, right fore.

The trot is a two-beat gait, the horse placing one diagonal pair of legs to the ground simultaneously and then springing, after a moment of suspension, on to the other diagonal. One beat is made as the left hind and right fore touch the ground and the second, after the briefest interval, as the opposite diagonal touches down.

The canter is a gait of three distinct beats, the horse leading with either the left fore – for the circle left – or the right fore – for circle right. In canter right the sequence is: left hind leg, then simultaneously, the legs of the left diagonal i.e. left fore and right hind, and finally the leading leg, right fore. This is followed by a period of suspension before the next stride is taken.)

Extending Work and Exercise Periods

Following the backing of the horse it is reasonable to extend the routine to include *two* work/exercise periods in the day. The first can be for up to twenty to thirty minutes in the arena, interspersed with frequent rest periods: the second may be the addition of an exercise period of an hour and upwards devoted to straightforward hacking in company with an older horse.

Lungeing and long-reining sessions are continued and in the former more emphasis is given to simple jumping exercises.

For safety's sake it is wise to have the horse on the lunge for a few minutes before riding him.

Riding Out

School work is a very necessary part of the young horse's education but it can be inhibiting, both physically and mentally. In any event it is not an end in itself but is rather a preparation for riding in the country outside the confines of the arena walls. Indeed, it used to be said that a day's hunting did more for the horse's balance and initiative than a month spent circling the school. Hunting is certainly the best way of unscrambling the problem horse who might have gone a bit sour as a result of the demands made on both body and mind by excessive schooling. Moreover, it does just as much for the rider. (Despite the efforts of a Government motivated by a mistaken concept of 'class', hunting is far from being over in the UK, even if it is carried on in altered form.)

However, for the young horse, hacking about the country, adjusting the balance to meet requirements of uneven ground, building muscle by uphill trotting and generally extending the young horse's outlook and experience is just as beneficial but without, of course, the infectious haroosh of the hunting field.

The value of an older, steady horse as a hacking companion is self-evident and it is particularly valuable when riding on roads and lanes where traffic is likely to be encountered. The older horse can then act as a shield for the youngster but it is also sensible to choose routes carefully and, where possible, to give the young horse the opportunity to watch traffic from safe vantage points before actually riding through it.

It is also essential to wear fluorescent clothing and use similar tack accessories. You may look like a Christmas tree but drivers do take notice and, one hopes, they slow down and give you a wide berth.

The more the young horse is ridden more or less on straight lines at walk and trot the better these gaits develop, although seemingly straight lines do not absolve the rider from changing the diagonal.

A happy picture of the young horse being ridden out with an older, steady companion.

Otherwise, keep a light, even contact with the mouth, without interrupting the natural carriage of the head, while riding him firmly from the legs and *in front* of them. He must be allowed to adjust his balance by using his head and neck as the balancing agent but at no time should he be allowed to slop along.

Take advantage of 'natural hazards', like a piece of shallow water or a small bank or log, through and over which the youngster can follow his older companion.

There will, too, be opportunities for the horse to learn how to carry himself at canter, a gait which so far will not have been included intentionally in his school work. The first canters need not be polished performances and it is probably wiser to choose a slightly uphill slope, for it is a potentially exciting gait that may induce an exuberant buck or two at the outset. Going uphill, the buck, if it comes, is not too uncomfortable and it is difficult for the horse to get his head down to deliver one of the really full-blooded, double-barrelled sort.

On the way home it is permissible to give short rest periods at walk on a lengthened rein, while still retaining contact with the mouth. The relaxation afforded is welcome for itself but it is also a way for the rider to express trust in his horse – and that is important.

Further Work on the Lunge

Starting to Canter

It should now be possible to introduce the canter into the lunge lessons and familiarize the horse with the rudiments of that gait. It will help establish the correct leads, or strike-offs, as well as developing the muscles of the back and quarters which are compelled by the three-time rhythm of the canter to work that much harder.

Nonetheless, cantering a circle is difficult and demanding and should be restricted to short periods, while the circle should be as large as possible.

Clearly, the side-reins have to be lengthened to allow for the altered posture or, indeed, removed altogether until the horse is comfortable in the gait.

The sequence of footfalls for canter left, for instance, are these:

1. Right (off) hind leg.

2. Right diagonal (off-fore and near-hind).

3. Left (near) foreleg, which is termed the leading leg.

Appreciating the sequence helps the trainer ask for the strike-off at the optimum moment.

The canter is obtained by first shortening the trot, driving the horse onto a hand that resists in a series of tweaks on the rein. It requires some experience to co-ordinate the driving action of the whip with the sympathetic rein action but being *aware* of what one is trying to achieve is a good start.

The trick then is to induce an increased inside bend, as though the circle was being reduced in size, and then to raise the head by just a little – don't overdo it lest the horse should hollow his back. The action is, indeed, momentary and is followed closely by asking for canter with whip, voice and body-language. Simultaneously, the rein has to be yielded to allow the inside shoulder to stretch into the final phase of the canter sequence. If the rein is fractionally late in yielding the shoulder is closed and the horse is unable to extend the foreleg fully.

It helps greatly if the trainer also moves in the rhythm of the canter, perhaps imagining riding the hobby horse of childhood.

If difficulty is experienced, a sure solution is to place a ground-pole across the track, one end in the corner of the arena and the other pointing towards to centre. The horse can then be asked to trot energetically into the corner and almost inevitably he will hop over the pole and land both in canter and on the correct lead.

Jumping on the Lunge

As an extension of the pole grid and the first small fence, and as an encouragement to greater activity and scope, the horse can be asked to jump small obstacles positioned on the long side of the arena.

It is sufficient, for the moment, to build the obstacles up to 60 cm (2 ft) high and for a spread fence to be of the same height and between 90–120 cm (3–4 ft) in width. Place a ground-pole just after the corner of the arena on the long side. Some 2.7 m (9 ft) away put up a pole supported on a block to give a 60 cm (2 ft) height. Trot the horse into this small fence and jump it from both directions, altering the disposition of the ground-pole and fence accordingly. To make a spread fence add a second pole and block alongside the first.

When the horse is jumping both happily and competently, a fence of cross-poles can be built between two uprights. Again, it need be no more than 60 cm (2 ft) high but it should have a ground-line (a pole on the ground close up to the fence). Place a pole from the ground to the top of the inside upright projecting some 45 cm (18 in) toward the landing side, so that the lunge line may pass smoothly over it and not get snagged on the upright. The pole will also act as an enclosing wing for the fence as well as a discouragement to any attempted evasion.

Canter Under Saddle

Towards the end of the primary school training the young horse will be strong enough to carry the rider for short periods at sitting trot which is the most effective schooling seat and, incidentally, a necessary preparation for the canter strike-offs.

To obtain a smooth canter strike-off, use is made of the corner of the school, which will encourage the horse in the correct bend and facilitate the transition. He has to be ridden actively into the corner at sitting trot, *without increasing the speed*, the bend being the equivalent to that recommended for the early trotting exercises, say that of a 15 m (50 ft) circle.

The Half-Halt

While the full use of the half-halt is not within the three-year-old's training programme, there is no harm in making use of it in a preparatory role in our endeavour to ride an acceptable canter strike-off, so long as we understand its implications.

In the most general sense the half-halt is a means of re-imposing balance within any of the gaits. Properly executed it results in a lightening of the forehand in response to more actively engaged hind legs and puts the horse in a posture from which he is better able to make a subsequent movement.

To execute the half-halt calls for an increase in the influence of the driving aids of back, seat and legs, even to the extent of bringing the shoulders slightly to the rear of hips but *without rotating the pelvis*. Almost simultaneous with the application of the driving aids, the hands are raised by a fraction and the fingers closed to prevent any increase in the speed. On the older, schooled horse the increased engagement of the hind legs, combined with the restraining lift of the hands, will cause the forehand to be raised and lightened. On the young horse we will not obtain a result of that standard, but it will have the effect of 'bringing the horse together' in preparation for the change of gait.

In perfection the whole operation is barely perceptible. With the young horse it has to be more clearly defined but *it must not be too strong* and on no account must the hands be brought to the rear in a backward pull. If the action of the aids is exaggerated the young horse is likely to react by 'shortening' his neck, while stiffening and hollowing his back, and that would never do.

Figure 37. The three-year-old in Primary School training will not show an outline as advanced as this but these drawings illustrate the aids for half-halt showing the influence of seat/body-weight, hands and legs.

Given that the preparatory half-halt produces an acceptable result, the rider enters the corner stretching the inside leg to weight the corresponding seat bone. Thereafter:

1. Outside leg is laid flat against the horse just behind the girth, while the *inside*, driving leg acts on the girth (see The 'Buttons' and Figure 38, pages 136–7).

2. The *inside* rein is raised fractionally and opened a little outwards while being supported by the outside rein.

3. To correspond with the advance of the horse's inside shoulder and hip, the rider must follow suit by advancing the *inside* seat-bone.

Faults in the Canter

Common faults preventing a smooth transition into canter are almost entirely connected to the rider's seat and posture, a matter which emphasizes the importance of the rider's competence. It is not enough for the rider, usually up to this point, the assistant, to be light, agile, agreeable and to produce the coffee at appropriate times. She needs also to be able to ride. If there is doubt on that score, the trainer can take over.

One most notable failing that can occur even with the experienced and above average rider is when the hands fail to yield sufficiently, or sufficiently quickly, as the horse makes the first stride. In consequence the action of the leading legs is restricted and the horse falls out of balance and becomes crooked, the quarters swinging outwards.

Mounted Jumping and the Grid

The first ridden exercises begin with a single ground-pole and then progress to a grid of first three and then five raised poles on the long side of the arena. The distance between the poles will have already been established when the exercise was practised on the lunge and it is important that it should be exactly right.

With the rider employing shortened stirrup leathers the horse can be ridden in a few circles to either hand at rising trot. When the movement is active and rhythmical, the horse dropping his nose, accepting the bit and relaxing the lower jaw, a wide turn is ridden from which a straight approach can be made to the grid.

A four-year-old horse crossing the pole grid actively, with lowered head and neck and a rounded top-line.

The grid is crossed in rising trot without alteration to the speed and rhythm but, of course, it demands increased flexion of the joints. The rider's legs act throughout in firm squeezes in time with the stride. Contact is

The more difficult exercise of trotting the grid when it is set on a circle. An excellent suppling/strengthening exercise.

maintained through relaxed elbows and hands moving forward to follow the stretching movement of head and neck.

The rider has to understand that accuracy in the approach and over the grid is paramount. Once the quality of the rhythm, contact or balance is lost, the work deteriorates and will be reflected in the horse's performance.

Other than a loss of rhythm, the usual failings in the grid exercise occur as a result of:

1. The rider losing contact by allowing the rein to slip through the fingers.

2. The trunk being inclined too far forward, i.e. in advance of the movement and thus out of balance with the horse.

(Indeed, this latter fault is a common cause of refusal, the rider jumping the fence, as it were, before having got there.)

The first jump is made by moving the last grid pole to double the trotting distance, say 3 m (10 ft) from the penultimate one and raising it to make a small fence between 45–50 cm (18–20 in). So long as the rider's legs remain active it should not present a problem.

Given that all goes well, it should be possible by the end of the primary training to jump an upright, spread and cross-pole fence of the same dimensions as those described in the lunge jumping exercise (p.127) and using the same distances and ground-poles. And that is quite sufficient at this stage.

Making use of the distance pole in the approach to a small cross-pole fence. The horse shows an excellent attitude.

Complete confidence over distance pole followed by a small bounce fence.

The Stiff Side

In the ridden flatwork it will be noticeable that the horse works more easily to one side than the other, usually going better on the left rein than the right. In brief, he has a 'stiff side' associated with his being crooked.

In almost every instance the problem is with the off-hind. Most horses have difficulty in flexing and engaging the hind legs and joints equally and they may often put the off-hind foot down outside and to the right of the corresponding forefoot. The matter is further exacerbated if the rider sits out of balance and is heavy in the use of the seat-bones. The resultant 'stiff side' causes the horse to lean on the opposite rein and against the rider's leg on that side.

Whatever we do, the condition will not disappear overnight and certainly not in the early training, but if we are aware of the problem we can make a start. It is, indeed, logical to begin the remedial action sooner rather than later, when it will have become confirmed.

Nor is there any point in trying to force the horse into bending the stiff side. Instead we have to ride at a good active trot, working the rein on the stiff side with the hand – the latter acting as though squeezing a rubber ball. The opposite rein is held in support, while the right leg acts to increase the engagement of the off-hind and its partner is held flat behind the girth in support. As always, it is the action of the rider's legs that is paramount.

In the secondary schooling we can go a stage further, circling the horse deliberately in the *wrong bend*. It is an uncomfortable business for the horse, although effective, but it would be premature to attempt the correction at this stage. (At the appropriate stage, the procedure is as follows. Employing an even contact, the horse is asked to describe the circle with an *outside* bend, i.e. the *wrong bend*. Because it is uncomfortable this corrective exercise must not be overdone, but after only a few circles he will slowly begin to give on the stiff side and accept the opposite rein.)

The Language of Riding

In Part 1 of this book, The Overview, the final paragraphs emphasized that the trainer of horses needs to develop particular qualities, as well as having an understanding of the physical and mental character of the horse. Finally, it is necessary to be more than just conversant with the *theory* of riding, if one is to be able to put it into practice.

At this juncture, midway between the primary and secondary schooling, it is worth reminding ourselves of the theory on which communication is based.

The essential mental *rapport* between horse and rider is a matter of experience, application and, perhaps as much as anything, the ability and willingness to listen with the body and the mind. It forms a large part of the communicative mode, but of equal importance is the rational system of signals made through the medium of the voice, the legs, the hands, and the disposition of the body-weight. The horsemen of the Renaissance called them the 'helps'; we use the term 'aids', further qualifying them with the word 'natural', the 'natural aids' being those applied through the body. When those physical actions are reinforced by whip and spur the latter are termed to be 'artificial aids'.

The effective use of these aids is the basis of the system of communication through which the rider is able to make requests of the horse and to influence the latter's posture and movement. They are the *language of riding* and the more fluent we become in the language the more easily will we obtain the results we want.

Sequence of the Aids

In every way the aids are inter-dependent, acting in concert and not in isolation. They operate in the sequence:

1. Prepare

2. Act

3. Yield

And they may, on occasion, be used to *resist* unwanted movements.

The *preparatory* aids are those used to secure the horse's attention and correct the balance before the rider asks for a specific response with the *executive* (acting) aid. To move from halt to walk, for example, the horse is alerted by a light squeeze of both legs, followed, almost simultaneously, by the closing of the fingers on the rein.

The horse is then ready for the aids to *act*. In this instance, the legs are applied positively on the girth, while the fingers open to allow the movement forward.

The aids *yield* the moment a response is obtained, and ideally a split second before that point, the release both of the leg pressures and the restraint of the hand telling the horse that he has done what was wanted.

It is all about good manners, the essence of *chivalry*, a word derived from the French *cheval*. In short, we have to remember to say 'Please' and 'Thank you', the words we learnt at our mother's knee – moreover, it works.

Finally, the aids may *resist* to combat an evasion. Hands may resist to restrain an over-impetuous forward movement, or a single leg can be used to counteract an unwanted shift of the quarters in one direction or another.

The Aid Combination

Very few of the riding manuals will include the *head* as one of the natural aids, and it is possible, if one considers the less than rational actions of some riders, that a percentage are unaware of its prime function in initiating physical movement.

It really is very necessary to ride with your head, to think in advance and to organize the horse before attempting a movement. The head needs to be engaged just as much as the horse's hind legs. Communicating with the horse on a mental plane is an acquired skill and no specific instructions are available that will lead to its attainment.

The *voice* is usually listed as the last of the natural aids, but is nonetheless an important one. However, it is an insufficiently sophisticated and subtle instrument with which to obtain more than a limited response. Furthermore, on pain of penalty points, one is forbidden its use in dressage tests, the dressage hierarchy not accepting it as a 'natural' aid – never mind that you are allowed to use spurs.

On the other hand the physical aids provide a system of communication that can reach a very high level of sensitivity and is capable of the most delicate gradation of expression.

Nonetheless, the effectiveness of this physical language of riding depends as much on the horse as the rider. Both of them require a compatible level of fluency, and before the horse can respond to the aids given by the rider he has first to be taught their meaning and the reactions expected of him. *Just as importantly, he needs to be physically capable of compliance, otherwise he becomes frustrated and confused.*

To summarize: unless both partners speak the same language and are, additionally, physically able to express their requirement on the one hand and to respond on the other, there are bound to be difficulties in the lines of communication.

The Legs

Paramount in the aid combination are the *legs*, the principal driving aid. Their purpose, whether used singly or as a pair, is to control the quarters and hind legs, the powerhouse behind the saddle. Through their agency the horse's hind legs are driven under the body to produce the propulsive thrust resulting in *impulsion*. The rider's legs also influence the quarters by holding them in place and preventing their deviation to one side or the other.

Function of the Single Leg

Each leg governs the movement of the corresponding hind leg. On the circle, the *inside* leg asks for the engagement of the horse's corresponding hind limb and is supported by its partner laid flat behind the girth to discourage the quarters from being carried off the track of the forelegs.

The optimum moment for applying the inside driving aid is when the horse's hind leg is just about to touch the ground. The leg is then engaged more vigorously and further under the body. Applied earlier or later its action is reduced to the point of negation. It follows that the rider has to 'feel' the position of the hind leg at any given moment. This necessary ability can be developed by practice. The movement, in fact, is 'felt' through the seat-bones when the rider has learnt to *listen*. A good exercise to develop the 'feel' is to have someone in the arena walk with the horse and call out as the hind leg is about to touch down.

In fact, it is possible to use the leg with great precision and effect. Conversely, its potential to confuse is immeasurable. Legs that swing about transmit unintelligible messages to the horse. To *speak* clearly and unequivocally they must be *still*, and a rider who has yet to acquire still legs should certainly never use spurs.

Legs – and hands, too – actually present something of a paradox, since both must be *still* and yet not be *immobile*. The leg moves in the sense that it responds to the movement of the horse's flank by being *supple* throughout its length. It cannot do that if it is tense and stiff.

The 'Buttons'

To obtain the best results the rider must be able to apply the legs in a number of prescribed pressures at particular points on the horse's body. Those points have been likened to a series of buttons set on a control panel fitted around the lower part of the girth (see Figure 38).

Of the four buttons A, the *impulsion* button, is the most important. It is situated at the rear edge of the girth and is activated by the leg exerting a smooth, inward-rolling squeeze against the lie of the coat. This forward-rolling squeeze is effective because is does not disturb the seat and it acts on the most sensitive part of body. Furthermore it complies with a rational method of riding. It is surely illogical to push *backwards* with the leg in order to go *forwards*.

Smoothness in the application of the aid is a paramount quality and results in a smooth response. Conversely, an abrupt action produces a corresponding response.

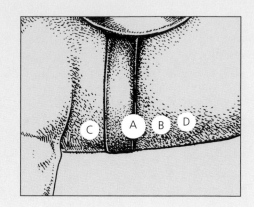

Figure 38. The control panel.

A is the all-important impulsion button.

B is used by the single leg to shift the quarters or by both legs in rein-back.

C is used, expertly, to encourage extension.

D is used in advanced movements as in piaffe, passage and for the flying changes.

The most heinous failing is for the toe to be turned outwards so that the back of the calf is in contact with the horse. It disturbs the seat and will certainly disturb the horse if a spur is worn. A glance at the back of the boot when one dismounts will reveal the extent of the failing. If the boot is marked beyond the central seam it can be taken that the rider has been riding from the calf with the toe turned out.

Button B, the point behind the girth is, with the exception of the aids for the rein-back, within the province of the single leg. Used singly, the leg is put on flat, with a direct inward squeeze. In conjunction with its partner its purpose is to:

1. Shift the quarters.

2. *Resist* any *unwanted* shift of the quarters.

3. Act to obtain lateral movement.

4. Assist as the outside leg in holding the quarters in changes of direction and at canter.

Both legs are used at B when asking for the *rein-back*.

From the outset there has to be a clear distinction between these two all-important buttons, A and B, if the horse is not to be confused.

The remaining two buttons are reserved for the advanced movements and do not enter into the primary and secondary schooling. Button D is used in flying changes, piaffe and passage; while Button C, in front of the girth, may be employed by the very expert to encourage greater extension, when it is applied by means of a surreptitious dig of the toe.

The Hands

The hands are the principal aids of restraint and in a supportive role help to govern the direction.

Their purpose is:

1. To receive the impulsion generated by the legs, which results in greater engagement of the quarters.

2. To regulate the energy thus generated, containing or releasing it to the required degree. (In the first instance there is a shortening of the base, in the second, an increase in the extension of the stride.)

3. To *re-channel* the energy, redirecting it to one side or the other.

Figure 39. The correct and therefore the most effective use of the aids to halt.

Figure 40. This is what happens when the aids are applied front to back from the hands.

For many riders the hands combine the functions of brake and steering wheel and no more. Taken a stage further we can regard and use the hands as the regulators of balance and outline. Indeed, the aim of the thinking rider is to find a balance between the driving aids at one end and the restraining hands at the other. The object is for the horse to move *within* the frame imposed by the two.

Figure 41. These are the aids applied to effect collection, which, of course, is not within the scope of the young horse but which the rider should understand when attempting to 'shorten' the horse.

Figure 42. Conversely, these are the aids applied to produce extension, or lengthening.

The most frequent error in modern riding is the predominance of hand over leg, riding from front to back, in fact. It is noticeable, even with advanced riders, when they seek to present an outline that will satisfy the dressage judges – although for the most part, one hopes, it does not go unrecognized by those worthies.

It occurs when over-dominant hands bring the head inwards, shortening the neck, so as to compensate for the lack of engagement in the quarters that would allow for a rounded outline. As a result the horse stiffens, while the movement is restricted and uneven. The horse becomes overbent, tucks his nose in and flexes in the upper-third of the neck rather than at the poll.

The rider, by relying on the hand, *forces the head to retreat towards the quarters instead of encouraging the quarters to advance to the head.*

Five Rein Actions

Hands certainly operate in a *preparatory* role by the momentary closure of the fingers combining with the brief squeeze of the legs. They *act* by the fingers opening to permit movement forward and, by closing, to restrain or *contain* it.

While it is appreciated that the hands are crucial in the changes of direction, it is not always understood that when they are applied in one of the five rein positions they are capable of governing and positioning both shoulders and quarters.

The five *rein actions* or *effects* may appear to be complicated and possibly irrelevant to the schooling of the young horse. In reality they are neither. Moreover, they have been appreciated, understood and practised ever since

Figure 43. Rein effects. From left: (a) Direct or opening rein; (b) indirect rein; (c) direct rein of opposition; (d) indirect rein of opposition in front of the withers; (e) indirect rein of opposition behind the withers – also known as the intermediary or intermediate rein.

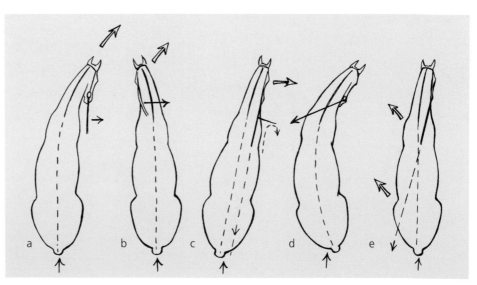

riding took the first tentative steps towards becoming a rational science. In fact, practical horsemen who may never have heard of the five rein effects are quite likely to practice them quite unconsciously.

In any event, the greatest benefit the rider obtains by understanding the five-fold rein combination is the ability to recognize the incorrect use of the reins that so often results in a contradiction of the movement required. When it occurs it is likely to cause the rider considerable frustration and confuse the horse more than somewhat.

The French school, always logical and analytical, is responsible for the nomenclature used and for the emphasis it gives to the rein and its effect. Other classical schools are well aware of the rein effects and certainly put them into practice, but it is the French who are responsible for the analysis and definition. The five rein effects generally recognized in academic equitation are these:

1. The direct or opening rein.

2. The indirect rein.

3. The direct rein of opposition.

4. The indirect rein of opposition *in front* of the withers.

5. The indirect rein of opposition *behind* the withers.

Direct reins act on the same side of the horse as they are applied. The *direct or opening rein* is applied by the hand being carried outward in the direction of the movement. It is used on turns and circles where the horse is bent to the inside and aligned to the direction of the movement.

Indirect reins influence the opposite side of the horse. The *indirect rein* is a neck rein, moving the opposite shoulder forward (i.e. the left indirect rein moves the right shoulder forward and to the right). It is used on turns and circles calling for the bend to be to the outside, as in the turn on the forehand, and it can also be used in a corrective capacity.

Reins of opposition block and re-direct the forward movement through the shoulder or the quarters or, in the fifth rein effect, through both.

The *direct rein of opposition* blocks the forward movement on the side to which it is applied. If, for instance, the right rein is used in this effect, the thrust from the quarters is blocked on the right side of the mouth. In consequence the quarters are shifted to the left. The rein is used in the fore-hand turn and, with both reins, in the rein-back, where the sustained forward movement is necessarily reversed.

Unhappily, it is this rein which is most frequently misused, particularly, of course, in the riding of turns and circles. To use an inside rein to effect a turn must, inevitably, cause the quarters to be moved outwards and off the track made by the forefeet. In that situation the rider has to seek to control the quarters through the outside leg, which is a contradiction of applied forces, the aids being used in opposition to each other!

The fourth rein effect, the *indirect rein of opposition in front of the withers*, moves the shoulders left or right according to the rein applied. The movement, however, produces a secondary one, which shifts the quarters in the opposite direction. It is a most effective rein to correct any deviation of the shoulder from the required track. Additionally, it will turn the horse on his centre (i.e. on the axis of a line vertically through the centre of the saddle), the bend being to the outside.

The last rein effect, the *indirect rein of opposition behind the withers*, is often termed *intermediary* or *intermediate*, so called because it comes between the third and fourth effects by acting on both shoulder and quarters. It is applied by the hand being directed towards the horse's opposite hip, and is further eulogized by the title the Queen of Reins. It is a rein effect of immense power and potential, moving the whole horse sideways and forward. It is used in leg-yielding and in the shoulder-in movement.

Warning

What is quite certainly unproductive is for a rein to be used in isolation rather than as part of a rein combination. Each rein is only made complete and effective when it is supported and complemented by its partner. Furthermore, the rein aids are subordinate to the leg aids and without ample, sustained impulsion no useful result is obtainable. The horse becomes, as it were, like a boat becalmed.

Up, Down and Sideways

Finally, a reminder of the permitted uses of the hands. Hands may move up and down on an arc. They may also move sideways. What they must not do is to be taken backwards or, which is equally heinous in the school context, a single hand must not be taken across the withers. In either event the movement is interrupted, affecting both balance and action.

Seat, Back and Weight

Finally, and central in every way to the aid combination, are the potent forces of the *seat* and *trunk* and the distribution of the *weight*.

Without doubt the upright, supple trunk combined with an open, spread seat in which there is no suspicion of tension in the muscles of the buttocks can be used as a powerful driving aid, so long as the hips always lead the movement. (Tension of the buttocks causes the seat to be raised and thus prevents the rider from sitting deep.)

However, over-emphasis of the driving character of the seat can prove decidedly counter-productive. There was a time when the Warmblood horses, before their development into the modern riding horse of quality, were often ridden in an unedifying back-seat driving position that would not be acceptable to a well-bred, sensitive horse.

The seat, with the hips leading the action, will, all else being equal, constitute the most effective of driving aids so long as the seat-bones push *upwards* and *forwards*. If they are driven *downwards*, the horse's back hollows to relieve the discomfort and both outline and action are lost.

Applied correctly, the seat, in concert with the braced or, more aptly, upward *stretched* back – the whole complemented by leg and hand – can produce a significant effect on both collection and extension by inducing increased engagement of the quarters.

In fact, in collection, the very slight inclination of the shoulders to the rear, altering the weight distribution, will encourage the horse to move his own weight further over his quarters so as to conform with the minimal alteration in the disposition of the rider's weight.

In lateral movements and changes of direction the horse is actually assisted by the rider weighting the inside seat-bone to complement the lateral shift of the horse's centre of gravity. Indeed, the very experienced will deliberately use the weight aid to put the horse in a position where it is he who must alter his centre of balance to conform with the altered distribution of the weight.

However, while the rider/trainer should understand the aids in the context of the theory implicit in correct, productive riding, do not expect too much of the young horse. Let the aids be positive but never forceful.

Trailer/Horsebox Drill

Entering and leaving trailers and horseboxes is a basic requirement of the modern horse.

There are some horses – happily, not too many – who throw the unexpected tantrum, or even refuse consistently when asked to enter the transport vehicle. They may be genuinely frightened, but in general the unreliable loader has either had a bad experience in the way of an uncomfortable ride or has suffered at the hands of a thoughtless and ignorant owner. (Some, again not too many, are bad travellers, a condition they share with dogs and humans. Most bad travellers manage better in a horsebox than a trailer and all seem to benefit from herbal or homoeopathic medication administered before a journey. The same is true of both dogs and people. The versatile *Arnica* can be used successfully and also, I believe, elm and walnut from the Bach Flower Remedies.)

It is certainly wise to include trailer/horsebox training as a specific part of the schooling programme, whether or not the young horse has been boxed as a foal, yearling or two-year-old.

The foundation for trouble-free loading is laid in the early lessons when the youngster is taught to walk in-hand. If the walk in-hand has been soundly established no trouble should be encountered, although every common-sense precaution has still to be taken to ensure that boxing is made easy for the horse and that no unnecessary difficulties are created.

The method is as follows:

1. When using a trailer, place the vehicle alongside a wall, so that at least one 'wing' is provided. That way 50 per cent of the danger of 'running out' is avoided.

2. Make sure the stabilizers are down so that the ramp is firm. Nothing upsets a horse so much as an unsteady footing.

3. Park the trailer with the front opened up and the ramp *facing the sun*, otherwise the inside will be a dark cavern and correspondingly discouraging for the youngster.

4. Move the central partition over to make the entrance wider and more inviting.

Having checked the detail meticulously, the *approach* can begin. The word is used advisedly since loading is not far removed from jumping so far as the initial phase is concerned. It is said, with every justification, that successful jumping is 50 per cent in the approach and 50 per cent about rider determination. Successful loading is not that much different.

After the work session, take a feed bowl in one hand and circle the horse in front of the vehicle at an active walk. If the left side of the vehicle is against the wall circle to the left and the opposite way in converse circumstances. This allows for the approach to be made from a slightly oblique angle and this in itself reduces the likelihood of a run-out.

Walking actively, make the approach off the circle with the assistant walking up briskly from behind. Show the horse the feed bowl as he puts his foot on the ramp and begins to walk up the ramp. Now, halt him in the box, give him his reward, make much of him and walk him straight out. This is less easy if there is no front unload facility and the horse has to come out backwards, but it can be accomplished if the trainer insists that he does so in a disciplined manner, taking one step at a time. Do, however, have the assistant in attendance at the side of the ramp to guide the quarters with a directing hand.

Repeat the exercise for a few days, reducing the reward to no more than a carrot or a mint. Then, with the breast bar in place, begin to secure the breeching strap and to put up the rear ramp, while, of course, the handler remains with the horse.

When the horse enters and leaves the vehicle quite happily, it is time to move it to different positions until finally he will load easily when it is placed in the centre of the yard.

Using a lunge line to encourage the reluctant loader.

Vigorous follow-up with the lunge line ensures a positive entry.

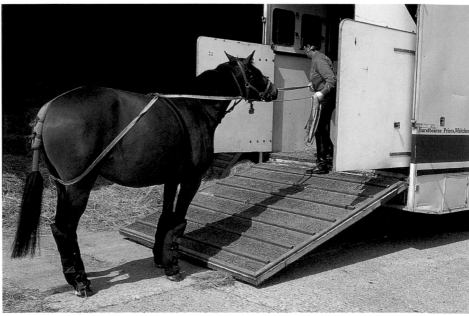

An improvized Galvayne's harness does not seem to arouse enthusiasm in this instance.

However, leave nothing to chance, and keep a lunge rein handy and attached to an appropriate point on the vehicle, so that the assistant can pass the rein behind the horse as an additional incentive to move forward should he evince any hesitation.

On occasions we may well have to manage single-handed and, against that time, it is wise to get the horse used to Galvayne's lead harness, the most useful loading tool described earlier in Part 2 – Additional Training Aids.

The horse needs then to become accustomed to short journeys and on these occasions can be accompanied by his companion. Obviously, great care should be taken to drive smoothly and steadily – one bad ride can put a horse off travelling for a long time.

Purpose can be given to the journeys by unloading at some pre-determined spot and taking the horse off for a ride before loading up again for the return home. Journeys can also be combined with a familiarization exercise, like going to a show or rally. The horse need not compete but he can be ridden or led about to give him experience of noise, bustle and potentially exciting conditions.

If introduced to the vehicle and travelling quietly and by gradual means, loading and unloading should become as routine and acceptable as being saddled and going for a ride; given, of course, that some b***** fool doesn't do anything totally stupid! (My old Thoroughbred horse is never led into the trailer. Instead, the stable door is opened and he loads himself on being asked to 'Get into your pram'. Only once has he not walked straight in of his own accord, and that was when I had omitted to put down the ramp! He was not amused and expressed his displeasure quite clearly.)

Turning Out

Primary school is completed towards the end of August or the beginning of September. The young horse is then 'turned away', a term that is by no means synonymous with being put out in a field to fend for himself.

The period between primary and secondary schooling is, in fact, just as important and demanding of time, thought, planning and management as the ridden work. Its purpose is to provide an opportunity for relaxation, albeit under supervision, and time for the young horse to develop naturally before the serious business of the secondary schooling begins in the following spring.

A safe, suitable paddock shared with a companion is an obvious priority. However, during the winter months the grass will be of little nutrient value until we have the first flush of spring growth and the youngster will need generous supplementary feeding to promote his development.

Theoretically, horses should manage under maintenance conditions on a generous ration of hay, but there is hay and hay and the nutrient value ranges from the highly nutritious to the nearly worthless and even worse than that. The mixture has, therefore, to be chosen with care (see Part 4 –

Nutrition) and, since one is feeding for growth, it needs to be supported with a daily non-heating concentrate feed as well as any vitamin/mineral supplement that may be appropriate.

Checks to be carried out before turning away include weight, examination of teeth and an assessment of the feet. In the last instance, the farrier can remove the shoes and trim the feet. If he thinks it necessary, have the horse fitted with 'tips' to prevent the feet from breaking up. *During the rest period the feet need to be examined at least once every six weeks.*

Otherwise, the golden rule is *supervision*. Both paddock and inmates need to be checked at least once a day and preferably twice.

PART 4

Secondary Education

Preliminaries and Objectives

The second phase in the education of the young horse begins in April of his fourth year.

If all has gone well he should by then have grown into a strong, well-developed young horse, but it would be unwise to put him straight into work. He needs to be prepared for it by gradual stages if sprains and strains are to be avoided.

Indeed, the first two or three weeks are best spent getting him used to a routine again. In any event he will need to be shod and generally tidied up. Worming programmes, injections, etc. have to be checked and his teeth need to be inspected. As a sensible precaution the physiotherapist might be asked to give him a look-over and he will certainly need to be weighed so as to determine an appropriate feed ration.

Thereafter, for upwards of a couple of weeks, time should be spent in a quiet recapitulation of the ground covered in the primary schooling of the first year. This is also an opportunity to check the fitting of all equipment and particularly that of the saddle. *Inevitably*, the latter will need adjustment or perhaps even replacement.

For the first lessons in the school it is better to restrict the work to the lunge exercises. In this way, the habit of obedience can be re-established without risk to the rider. It is indeed likely that the horse will attempt to assert himself in the occasional expression of high spirits and it is better for him to do so on the lunge than under saddle.

In any event, there will be moments of resistance and occasional rebellion in the secondary stage of schooling. Other than the odd buck and a jump for sheer *joie de vivre*, the principal cause of resistance arises from the nature of the work asked of the young horse.

In the primary schooling it was sufficient for him to carry out movements obediently and as best as he was able, allowing for his state of development. Now, as he is stronger and much improved in his outline and muscle structure, he will be asked to perform with greater energy and effort. In plain terms, he is asked to *work* and this marks the watershed between the primary school and the secondary education. (It is not really that much different in the human context.)

The work, in parts, does involve real effort and concentration and it is a fact that most horses will prefer the easy and less demanding way. When pressed to work they will seek ways of evasion rather than submit gracefully to the greater physical effort. A good trainer, aware of the problem, will overcome the difficulties with firm, but sensitive riding while appreciating that the horse can do no more than is within the limits of his physique.

I suspect, however, that a great many horses, for whatever reasons, do not get much further than an 'advanced primary level'.

The overall objective of the secondary education is the production over a period of about eight months, say up to December, of a well-conditioned all-round riding horse within reach of his maximum potential. He should be able to jump plain and coloured fences reliably and to perform more than adequately across country. He needs to have learnt his manners, in and out of the stable, and to be safe in traffic.

Along the way to this desirable state there are subsidiary, overlapping objectives to be attained. It is as well for them to be defined and for us to bear them in mind.

1. Progressive physical conditioning, which comprises the three prime elements: *grooming*, *feeding* and *exercise* in the correct measure and balance.

2. Continued emphasis on the horse's mental development. An obedient horse, submitting willingly to the rider's aids, is certainly of prime importance, but neither of these criteria should be obtained at the expense of the horse's natural initiative. We want a thinking horse (although preferably one thinking on the same lines as ourselves), not a press-button automaton.

3. Placing the horse in hand and into increasing acceptance of the bit.

4. Consolidating the reception of the aids up to the secondary standard.

5. Increase of both *lateral* and *longitudinal* suppleness through gymnastic exercises.

6. Inducing a greater degree of straightness in the horse.

7. Continuing and extending the jumping training.

8. Ensuring reliability in traffic by greater exposure to varied road conditions.

9. Making the first introductions to the double bridle.

Nutrition

Central to the training, and, indeed, to the ownership of a horse, is the animal's feed intake in terms of quantity and constituents related to the work expected of him. Trainers, riders and owners cannot expect to have the knowledge of the qualified dietician, even if they are more than qualified in terms of practical experience, but they need to know a bit more than the information printed on the bag and that entails a good understanding of the principles involved.

Food is utilized to provide for the four basic requirements of life. They are:

1. To maintain body temperature.

2. To replace natural wastage of the tissue (if the food intake is insufficient to fulfil these essential needs, death ensues).

3. To build up body condition.

4. To supply energy required for movement and for the internal purposes of digestion, circulation, etc.

Of the four requirements the first two are paramount and when the food intake is markedly insufficient they will be maintained at the expense of the others. The body can lose condition (i.e. become thin) and lose the energy, or strength, for movement over a basic level without death occurring. In that situation the greater proportion of the food intake will go to maintaining body temperature, less will be employed in the interest of body condition and the horse loses weight in consequence.

The imposition of hard work, demanding a high level of energy output, on a horse in receipt of a low maintenance diet will produce the same result. In that instance, the expended energy demands a larger share of the feed intake; body temperature and tissue replacement, prime essentials to the continuance of life, must still have their share and so precious little is left for body condition.

Simplistically, the intake would be insufficient to sustain condition as well as supply the energy needed to meet the increased workload. Taken to its conclusion, the body, after becoming weak and listless, would lose the capacity to replace tissue, the temperature would drop and the animal would die.

In an opposite situation, where the food intake was in excess of the demands made of it, the body condition would increase and the horse becomes fat.

First Principles

When the natural diet of the feral horse is replaced in domestication by one using harvested and preserved feedstuffs, it follows that the latter should replicate the same balance and constituents and be fed as nearly as possible in the manner in which the animal would naturally consume the feed intake.

In fact, in nature, the horse feeds slowly and almost continuously from ground level. Once the stomach is about two-thirds full, food is passed into the intestines to continue the digestive process.

Ideally, the stabled horse, who in domestication retains exactly the same digestive system, should be fed in similar fashion, being given a handful of food every five minutes from a container placed on the ground. Since that is clearly impractical, he needs to be given feeds small enough not to overload the stomach's capacity, and to be given them at frequent intervals. In fact, *feed little and often* is the inviolable rule, since the stomach is small in relation to the animal's overall size. Its capacity and the ability of the digestive system to cope with the food intake is not more than 1.8 kg (4 lb) or so of concentrate feed in total at one time and feeds should not exceed this weight. Hay, providing bulk that aids the digestive process, can be given in larger quantities because it is eaten more slowly. The main portion of the hay ration is given at night when the horse has more time to eat and digest it.

Consequences of Excess

Horses tend to eat their rich and not easily digestible short feeds rapidly. If they were to receive one or two large feeds rather than three or four small ones, the capacity of the stomach would be too small to contain the volume. The stomach would then become distended, preventing the muscles assisting the digestive process from working to that end: the food would ferment, giving off gases and causing such acute pains as might rupture the stomach. The condition is made more likely by the horse's inability to vomit.

The prospect of exercising the horse too soon after a feed gives rise to another principle: *do not work immediately after feeding*. The stomach is situated behind the diaphragm, a section of muscle separating it from the chest cavity proper. The diaphragm is in contact with the lungs in front, and at the back almost touches the stomach and liver.

After a feed the stomach and the intestines (which will still be digesting the previous meal) will become distended and the stomach will press against the diaphragm. This is of no consequence while the horse is at rest but, were he to be exercised immediately, the effort involved would cause him to expand the lungs and breathe more deeply. The expansion of the lungs would then exert pressure on the elastic structure of the diaphragm which, in turn, would press against the distended stomach. The breathing would, obviously, be impaired along with the ongoing digestive process. Painful indigestion would be caused and it might well become so acute as to develop into a severe case of colic. At its worst – that is if fast work were to be carried out on a full stomach – the lungs would become choked with blood and a rupture of the stomach would be likely to occur.

Dietary Constituents

The constituents comprising a *balanced* diet are the following, and feed manufacturers will usually define the percentages contained in packaged feeds.

Protein

Protein acts to:

1. Assist in the formation of body tissue.

2. Replace muscular wastage.

3. Provide the enzymes that assist with the utilization of energy.

Fats and Carbohydrates

In simple terms these are producers of energy and foods containing these elements are *necessary* to the working horse. Protein, however, is *essential*. Feedstuffs given to horses do not usually consist entirely of protein or of fats, or of carbohydrates in the form of starch and sugar, but the other constituents are valueless as producers of energy unless protein is also present. Too much starch and sugar makes the protein element difficult to digest.

Ratios of Fats, Carbohydrates and Protein

Fats produce $2\frac{1}{3}$ times more heat/energy than starch and sugar.

The desirable ratio between protein and starches and sugar is 1:10 in a horse not in work on a maintenance diet. It rises by four times or more when the animal is in medium/hard work.

The proportion of fat to protein is in the area of 1:2.5.

Overfeeding produces excess fat which is not conducive to athletic activity and is, moreover, uneconomical.

A surplus of protein will also overload the system to the point of breakdown, affecting circulation and liver function and causing diarrhoea, while it may also be responsible for deviant behavioural problems.

Water

Water is as essential to life as solid food and, indeed, the horse's body consists of 80 per cent water. Horses, it used to be estimated in the military context, could survive thirty days without food but for only about a quarter of that time without water.

To be fully utilized all foods must pass into the system in solution and, without water, the natural process of the body and digestion must break down. Water is present in dry foods at a level of about 10–12 per cent, while root crops may contain as much as 70 per cent.

We can forget the old adage about watering before feeding, recognizing that *water should always be available*.

Fibrous Roughage

Hay (or its modern counterpart, haylage) is the essential bulk constituent, forming between one-half and two-thirds of the stabled horse's diet, but fibrous roughage exists to a degree in all vegetable foods.

Bulk foods are necessary to the digestion of herbivores and, in particular, they assist in breaking up the concentrates in the diet, ensuring their absorption into the system.

Hay can be available in a variety of forms of different nutrient value. The prime division is between *meadow* and *seed* hay. The first is made from fields laid permanently to grass, while the latter is grown on arable land as one of a rotation of crops. In both instances the quality depends on the quality of the land on which it is grown and then on how the crop was made.

Meadow hay, the softer of the two, is more readily digestible and contains a greater variety of grasses. It is very suitable for young stock and for horses in light to medium work. In practice it is usually worthwhile to mix meadow hay with the harder seed hay.

Seed hay contains a higher percentage of clovers and of the two is more suitable for horses in hard work. It is more expensive but it is also more nutritious. However, it is less digestible and needs to be fed with discretion.

Both types should be cut when the grasses are in flower, much of the nourishment being in the flower and the seed. A good hay mixture of red clover and rye grass will contain as much as 12 per cent protein and have a protein/starch ratio of 1:4. Hay cut when the flower has gone to seed has a very much lower nutrient level.

Good hay should be greenish in colour and smell sweet. The grasses need to be in flower and when the bale is opened the hay is springy to the touch.

Hay should not be dusty or show mould spores. That which has got wet after turning will be susceptible to mould and is to be avoided. Musty hay, stacked or baled before it is dry is not for horses. Most will sensibly refuse it and those who do eat it suffer from distended bellies and colic. 'Mow-burnt' hay, which has been stacked too soon, heated in consequence and become brown is also to be avoided.

Once, in days gone by, much store was set on buying 'old' hay rather than that 'newly' made. Old hay was reckoned to be between six and eighteen months old, when it was thought to be in the best condition. Before six months it was held to be too soft to promote hard condition and after eighteen months it was well past its best. However, the forage trade ruling was that hay in Europe became 'old' after Michaelmas Day, September 29.

Today, one just buys the best hay available and is ruthless in one's rejection of the second-rate, which does not always endear one to the vendor but is, one hopes, appreciated by the horse.

It is now accepted practice to soak hay (but not haylage, of course) before feeding. However, such dust and mould spores as may be present will not be removed by a quick sluice under the tap. Hay needs to be soaked for at least ten to fifteen minutes but no longer, lest the nutrients go out with the spores. It is then drained before being fed.

Hay is best fed from the ground, conforming to the natural way of things, but this is wasteful and it is difficult to be certain how much has been eaten and how much trampled underfoot. However, I do not like hay racks (which cause the horse to eat the contents like a giraffe and increasing the likelihood of seeds falling into the eyes), preferring a small mesh net at which the horse can pick.

Alternatively, the modern way is to feed *haylage*, made from grasses packaged in vacuum-sealed polythene bags. It is highly nutritious and on that count allows a considerable reduction in the feeding of concentrates, but it is expensive. Nonetheless, it is claimed that horses can go hunting on nothing more and it is certainly dust-free.

Minerals

Minerals are present throughout the body. Their broad purpose is to control the constant changes taking place in the body and they are necessary for the maintenance of life. Continual replacement of minerals is necessary and is made through constituents of the food intake.

While all minerals are classified as micro-nutrients, in that they are required in vastly lower quantities than major feed items, they are further classified as macro-minerals (required in *relatively* large quantities) and trace minerals (required in only minute quantities, but still important to the horse's well-being).

The major minerals required are:

Calcium – for bone structure, blood, heart, nerve and muscle function and, in mares, lactation.

Phosphorus – for bone growth, protein synthesis and adaptation for body use of carbohydrates and fats.

Sodium – usually sourced from sodium chloride or common salt – for control of fluid balance, transfer of nerve impulses and other metabolic and muscle functions.

Potassium – for regulation of body fluid, nerve and muscle function and uptake of carbohydrates.

Sulphur – connected with synthesis of amino acids, hoof growth and enzyme activity.

Magnesium – for nerve and muscle function, formation of bones and teeth, regulation of calcium:phosphorus ratios, enzyme activation and metabolic processes.

Important trace elements are:

Cobalt – a component of Vitamin B12 and involved in the growth/replacement of red blood cells.

Iron – for production of red blood cells and the formation of haemoglobin.

Copper – for formation of haemoglobin and various body tissues.

Manganese – for normal tissue growth, reproduction and lactation.

Zinc – for metabolism of carbohydrates and fats, and for general growth.

Iodine – for correct functioning of the thyroid gland, growth and reproduction.

Vitamins

Vitamins are organic compounds required only in minute quantity but nonetheless essential to correct physiological functions. The two broad categories are fat-soluble vitamins, including vitamins A, D, E and K, which can be stored in the liver, and water-soluble vitamins, including vitamin C and the B complex, which cannot be stored. Generally speaking, they can be derived from a variety of natural sources, but some processes in the production of feedstuffs can deplete natural levels. The absence of specific vitamins from the diet can result in various problems including bone disorders, nervous affections, rickets, sterility, low resistance levels, etc.

Proportions of Bulk to Concentrate

While there are differences in the details of equine nutrition, there is no disagreement about the long-established rule relating to the bulk/concentrate ratio:

Horses in light work should be fed in the proportion of two-thirds hay (bulk) to one-third concentrate or 'short' feed.

Horses in medium work (hunting, regular competition) will operate more effectively on a 50/50 ratio.

Horses in hard work (top-level competition, etc.) may have the hay ration reduced to one-third of the total intake.

In the present context the young horse may be assumed to be in light work, possibly moving towards medium at the end of the secondary schooling. At whatever stage, 'green' feed, which may be said to encompass carrots and the like, provides succulence and variety to the feed and is usually consumed with relish.

Having settled on a suitable ration, let it be approached by gradual stages. If a point is reached at which the horse is becoming too boisterous in his behaviour, adjust the ration accordingly to incorporate non-heating constituents. There is no sense at all in trying to teach a horse who is so full of himself that he cannot listen.

Developing Work and Exercise

The routine remains based on two work/exercise periods a day and allows for 'playtime' when the horse relaxes in the paddock.

The work period, with frequent rest intervals, will be between half and three-quarters of an hour while the exercise period, devoted to hacking, will extend to an hour and a half or more. Most trainers, but not all, prefer to exercise in the morning, reserving the school work for the afternoon. At this time, both grooming and strapping become increasingly vigorous.

The Gaits

The three basic school gaits; walk, trot and canter are all practised in the primary curriculum. Now it is time to appreciate the sub-divisions of each gait, all of which contribute to increased suppleness, obedience and overall control.

Walk

There are four sub-divisions to the walk: *medium, collected, extended* and *free*.

Medium walk is a free, active march movement in a distinct four-beat rhythm with moderate extension, i.e. the hind feet touch the ground *in front* of the prints made by the forefeet.

Medium walk.

Medium walk performed by a five-year-old of different conformation.

Collected walk represents the ultimate in the gait and will not be attained in secondary training, but that is no reason for not working towards the goal of collection. It is marked by a shortening of the outline as a result of a shortening of the base of support. The horse should move resolutely forward with noticeable impulsion from engaged hind legs and strongly flexed hocks. The hind feet touch the ground somewhat *behind* the prints of the forefeet. The neck is raised and arched, with the head held near the vertical plane.

In *extended* walk the horse covers as much ground as possible with each stride while maintaining the regular four-beat rhythm. The hind feet touch the ground *noticeably in advance* of the prints of the forefeet. The horse remains in positive contact with the bit but head and neck are extended.

Free walk is a form for relaxation, for example after a period of intensive work. The outline is lowered and extended with head and neck stretched.

Collected walk with the base line shortened.

Free walk with the outline lowered and extended.

Trot

As with the walk, there are four recognized sub-divisions of the trot, which is a two-beat gait. Trot at this stage is obtained from walk, following an initial preparatory half-halt.

Working trot is probably the most productive of the schooling gaits, lying between *medium* and *collected* in the trot spectrum and inclining more to the latter. The hind feet touch down a little *behind* the print of the forefeet.

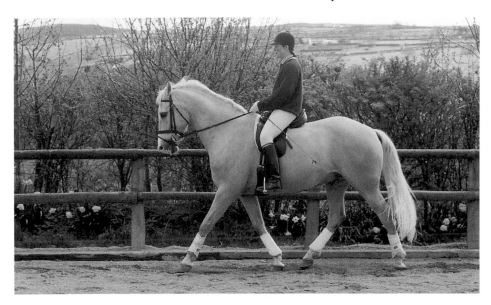

Working trot – active with good impulsion and engagement of the hind leg.

The five-year-old in a very creditable working trot.

Medium trot is between *extension* and *collection*, inclining toward the former. It is rounder than the extended form, but with noticeable engagement of the hind legs. The hind feet touch down *in* the prints of the forefeet.

Collected trot is not within the secondary schooling but we should be aware of the requirements. In this form the stride is shortened and noticeably elevated and, as in collected walk, the hind feet fall *behind* the prints of the forefeet. The head is close to the vertical with neck raised and arched.

Medium trot – vigorous, forward-going. Note the driving position of the rider's leg.

Collected trot – with notable elevation.

Extended trot covers as much ground as possible with a *lengthened* stride. It is *not* a question of taking hurried strides. While maintaining the same rhythm, the steps are lengthened because of an increased engagement of the hind legs induced by the rider's driving legs. The horse remains 'on the bit' but the hands allow the neck to lower and extend so as to avoid elevation.

Approaching the extension but not quite there yet.

Engagement behind ensures a brilliant floating extension.

The extremes in the trot spectrum are represented by *collection* and *extension*. *Working* trot lies slightly to the collected side of the centre line, while *medium* comes closer to extension.

In the secondary phase the rider will be able to make use of the sitting trot as the horse's back becomes stronger, but must always be prepared to rise to the trot if the horse seems to stiffen under the seat.

Canter

The sub-divisions at canter are: *collected*, *working*, *medium* and *extended*. The gait is one of three beats, the horse leading with the left fore on circle left and vice-versa.

Collected canter, again not within the remit of the secondary stage, asks for the horse to be 'on the bit' with head raised and the neck arched. Clearly, the quarters are strongly engaged and there is noticeable lightness of the forehand. The outline and the strides are shortened but the horse is highly mobile and the impression is one of great lightness.

Working canter – the gait form between collected and medium.

The chestnut five-year-old in an impressive working canter.

Working canter lies between collected and medium.

Medium canter is, in terms of stride length, between working and extended. It is thus reasonably extended and the propulsive thrust of the quarters is in evidence. Again, the horse is 'on the bit' but the head is carried a little in advance of the vertical and both head and neck are lower than at working canter and lower again than in the collected form.

Extended canter has the stride covering as much ground as possible and there is noticeably strong impulsion in the quarters. Still 'on the bit', the horse lowers and stretches out the head and neck carrying the face in advance of the vertical.

above Medium canter with reasonable extension.

above right Collected canter with shortened outline.

right Extended canter in the moment before the head is lowered and the foreleg extended. The rider has momentarily lost her exemplary leg position but the powerful engagement of the horse's hind leg is notable.

Counter-canter is a suppling and balancing movement in which the horse is asked to canter to the left whilst on the right lead and vice versa. It is not included in the secondary education.

Half-halt in canter showing clearly how the horse is re-balanced on the quarters.

Almost at the moment of suspension in the canter gait.

Magnificent energy and activity in this medium canter and a very obvious 'uphill' outline.

School Figures and Free Forward Movement

The physical exercises performed in the school rely on the accurate riding of the school figures. Their purpose is to strengthen and supple the body, improving the overall balance and the straightness of the horse. They are based on the circle and elements of the circle referred to in Changes of Direction and Changes of Stride Length and Outline, in Part 3.

Circles

The correctly ridden circle is, indeed, the key to the suppling and balancing movements which form the school discipline. In reality, very few of us ride good circles and it follows that the same is true of the horses. It does, however, help us to avoid the ovoid if the circles are marked out in sawdust or something similar.

In the early secondary schooling it is sufficient if we can ride the horse through the corners in four quarter-circles of a 15 m (50 ft) diameter and perform 20 m (66 ft) circles pretty accurately to describe the figure-of-eight, the changes through the circles and simple loops and serpentines. Ten-metre circles are beyond the horse at this early stage and will not be within his compass until the secondary education is further advanced towards the end of the year.

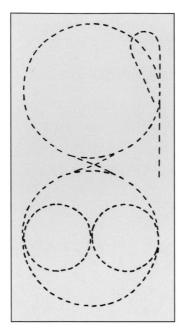

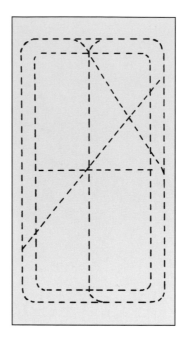

Figure 44. A selection of school figures that can be practised with great advantage. The diagram shows the circles and changes of hand (direction).

Figure 45. Further possible changes of hand that can be made within the school. The inside dotted line represents the 'inside' track, 2 metres (6ft 6in) from the wall.

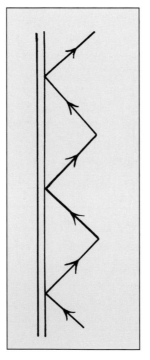

Figure 46. The zigzag. A useful figure to ride when teaching obedience to the action of the single leg.

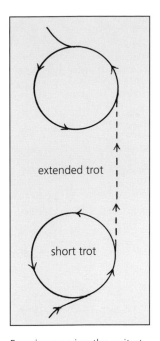

Exercises varying the gait at trot and canter

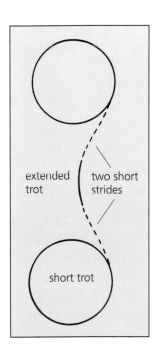

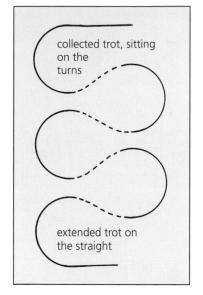

SERPENTINE

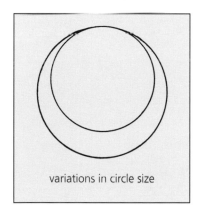

variations in circle size

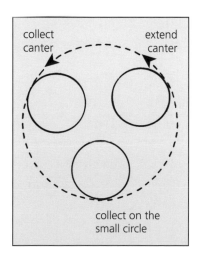

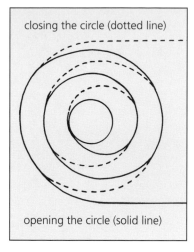

SPIRAL

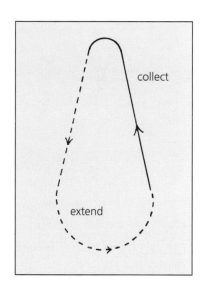

Figure 47. Various useful school figures.

169

Free Forward Movement and Rhythm

As always, the degree of success achieved in the school figures and the specific movements depends on the horse moving *forward* willingly and with sufficient impulsion to make it necessary to exert a modicum of restraint. Additionally, we look for an improvement in the *rhythm*, and that does not come about until the horse accepts a steady, equal and very light contact with the hands. (Resist any temptation to tighten the grip on the reins, instead imagine you are holding a baby bird in the hand and ride just a shade slower than the speed at which the horse can maintain his balance.)

Most horses will at some point give the impression of holding back rather than making an immediate response to the legs. Some may, indeed, come off the bit altogether, rejecting the contact and even retracting the nose to come 'behind the bit' (The horse is 'on the bit' when he accepts the contact with the head held nearer to the vertical than otherwise and is properly engaged behind and in true self-carriage. He is 'above the bit', horrid thought, when his mouth is thrown upwards above the level of the hands. In that extreme position he is also out of control.)

For the most part, the evasion is a feeling of 'holding off' and it may be an attempt by the horse to assert himself. Otherwise it can arise as a result of irritation or resentment and, if the horse is stiff from overwork or because of some physical weakness, he will certainly be reluctant to comply with the requests made of him. Finally, it might just be a case of *old-fashioned laziness*. In that event do *not* repeat the leg aid but use the whip in a couple of firm taps behind the girth.

Exercises

Halt

The fundamental riding requirement is contained in three words: *Start-Steer-Stop* and, having obtained the first two, it is as well to work on the last in the early stages of the secondary training. The horse should have been accustomed to halting squarely in hand and on the lunge and will have been acquainted with the half-halt in the last weeks of the primary training. Work on the half-halt should now be extended until it can be practised during the school sessions up to half-a-dozen times in the course of riding a circuit of the arena.

The half-halt prepares the horse for the full halt, which is no more than an extension of the latter, the intermittent restraining aids being applied a little more strongly until the horse stops. However, the legs must be kept on when the rein is *relaxed* (it is not 'given'). Thereafter, the legs relax but remain in contact with the horse. The key word in the giving of the aids is *intermittent*. If either hand or leg is clamped on unremittingly, the horse is driven into resistance and a smooth, balanced halt becomes impossible.

The usual failing in halt is for the horse to trail a hind leg. It is countered by the action of the rider's leg on the same side so as to bring the hind leg forward, or by asking for the halt on a curve i.e. to the left if the left hind is trailed and vice versa.

Halt. Square and in balance.

The chestnut's effort at halt is not square, which is a common failing. However, he is attentive.

A foreleg too far under the body can be corrected by easing the rein on that side and giving a little push with the corresponding leg.

If the halt really goes to pieces it is no good trying to correct it at that juncture; instead ride forward and try again.

Turn on the Forehand

This is an unnatural turn for the horse but of enormous importance in his schooling. Indeed, the turns on the forehand and quarters represent the watershed between the partially schooled horse and the trained one.

The natural way for the horse to turn, whether through 90 degrees or even 360 degrees, is on his centre, when he moves round the vertical axis at the girth. Occasionally, a startled horse may perform something like a turn on the quarters, when the forehand is moved round the pivot provided by the latter, *but he never turns the opposite way, on his forehand.*

The basis for the movement is the 'move-over' stable drill, taught early in the primary training. The reasons for teaching the turn under saddle are these:

1. When the quarters are moved to one side or the other in response to the action of the rider's single leg it is necessary for the hind legs to be lifted and crossed. It is, therefore, a means of suppling and strengthening the individual hind legs, improving joint flexion and increasing the power of the all-important loin.

2. A rider who has the ability to move the quarters at will also has the ability to prevent any *unwanted* shift and is, on that account, in a position to *straighten* the horse.

3. Mobility of the quarters also contributes to mobility of the jaw and the ability to obtain flexion on either side of the mouth (see The Stiff Side, p132). It is the initial and essential introduction to the lateral work. Without being able to perform the forehand turn one is not within reach of an acceptable half-pass.

4. On a far less exalted level it is impossible to open a gate with quiet competence unless the horse understands the turn on the forehand. (For myself, this is as good a reason as any for teaching it.)

Teaching from the Ground
The turn is first taught from the ground, the trainer standing at the horse's head, facing the rear, and tapping with the whip behind the girth. Within a

couple of days it should be possible to make the turn from a walk, the trainer, perforce, walking backwards with the assistant following up. The horse is then checked with the rein and the quarters moved over with the aid of the tapping whip before the walk is continued on the new line of direction. Of course, the movement has to be practised in both directions.

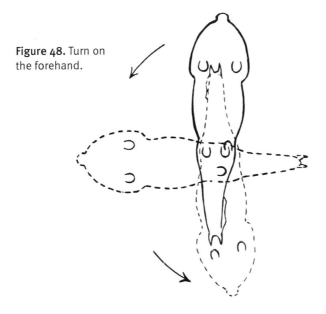

Figure 48. Turn on the forehand.

Teaching from the Saddle

Before attempting to teach the turn from the saddle the rider needs to be very clear about the aids to be employed. Incorrect combinations of leg and hand only serve to confuse the horse and anything approaching the contra-dictory will effectively prohibit the execution of the movement.

The turn is approached from the usual active walk. The horse is checked (half-halt) and brought to the square halt. To move the quarters to the right, the left leg is laid flat on the horse behind the girth (position B – see Figure 38, p137) and pushed inwards. (The digging heel and turned out toe are to be resisted as a certain way of upsetting the horse's composure). The right leg is held ready to limit any excessive movement.

The left rein, in concert with the leg aid, is used in the fifth effect, the indirect rein of opposition (to the haunches) behind the withers, in which the rein is placed carefully towards the right hip, the right rein being eased to permit the head to be turned slightly to the left. Both aids act simultaneously and intermittently. Unbroken pressure in either department will be unproductive, causing a reciprocal resistance.

Turn on the fore-hand in which the horse moves the quarters round the forelegs.

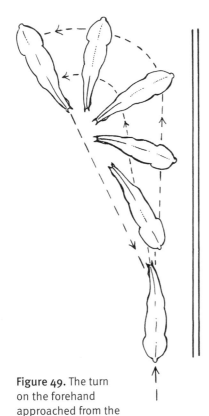

Figure 49. The turn on the forehand approached from the reverse half-volte.

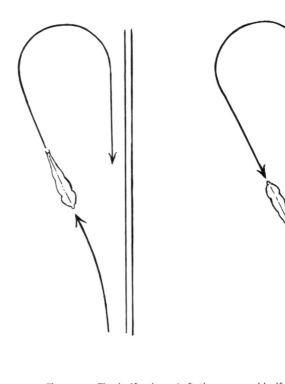

Figure 50. The half-voltes. *Left:* the reversed half-volte used to teach the turn on the forehand.
Right: the half-volte from which the turn on the quarters (see page 181) can be approached.

Reverse Half-volte

A useful school figure in teaching the turn through 180 degrees is the reversed half-volte (see Figure 50). It involves no more than leaving the track and returning to it, turning about by means of a 6 m (20 ft) circle. Following the preparatory half-halt, the same aids as above are applied and, hey presto!, the horse takes his quarters round his forehand. At least that is what he will do so long as the rider does not 'try too hard' and increase the measure of the aids in consequence.

Leg-yielding

This is the easiest of the school movements, a valuable one and a natural follow on from the forehand turn, since the same lateral aids are employed, but in this instance to move the whole body away from the rider's active leg.

The exercise begins at walk, taking advantage of the *inside* track on the long side of the arena. (The inside track is some 2 m (6 ft 6 in) inside the arena's perimeter and parallel to it.)

The movement is much helped by the gravitational pull of the arena rails. Being a creature of habit the horse is always happy to return to the familiar outside track and will, indeed, need little persuasion to move back to it.

From the active walk on the inside track on the right rein, for example, the horse is moved sideways by the right leg and right indirect rein of opposition supported by the left rein being carried slightly outwards to emphasize the required direction. This left rein a) prevents the bit sliding through the the mouth and b) checks any tendency for the neck to be overbent to the right when only a slight flexion is needed. The left leg is used on the girth at position A to maintain impulsion and, if necessary, to counter any excessive movement of the quarters.

Leg-yielding. The horse moves from the inside track outwards to the rails.

Leg-yielding need not, of course, be confined to the school; it can be practised when out hacking, the horse being moved into and away from the side of the roadway.

Within a week the horse should be capable of yielding in either direction at trot without interruption to the rhythm: once more, so long as the rider does not try too hard.

Shoulder-in

Perfected by the greatest of the eighteenth-century Masters, François Robichon de La Guérinière, this movement has become acknowledged as the ultimate suppling exercise, increasing the engagement of the individual hind legs and the flexion of the leg's three joints. Moreover, once perfected, it gives the rider a very high degree of control over the horse and leads to both straightness and collection.

Conversely, it is worthless and counter-productive when performed incorrectly. For these reasons the rider has to have a clear understanding of what the shoulder-in seeks to accomplish and of the execution of the exercise.

The official definition given by the FEI (the International Federation) is this: 'The horse is slightly bent round the inside leg of the rider. The horse's inside foreleg passes and crosses in front of the outside leg; the inside hind leg is placed in front of the outside leg. The horse is looking away from the direction in which he is moving.'

The use of the word 'bent' is still possibly misinterpreted. It does not imply that the *spine* is bent since, as mentioned earlier, that is possible to only a minimal degree. What is meant is that, in the making of a turn, or in the shoulder-in movement, the impression is given of the horse being bent round the rider's leg because the muscles on the inside of the body are flattened while those of the opposite side are stretched and assume a greater prominence.

The basic shoulder-in is performed on three tracks (i.e. the tracks formed by the outside hind, the inside hind and outside fore together, and the inside hind). The four-track version (in which each leg follows a separate track) does not apply to secondary schooling, only being within the capability of the very supple advanced horse.

Aids for Shoulder-in

The movement is approached off the circle (see Figure 51). The inside leg acts actively on the impulsion button to push the outside shoulder along

Shoulder-in with the quarters held square in relation to the rail and the movement led by the outside shoulder.

The young chestnut horse has his own more flamboyant version of the shoulder-in but it is correct enough and the head-carriage is particularly pleasing.

Figure 51. Shoulder-in, the ultimate suppling exercise. Here the movement, shoulder-in to the right, is made off the circle.

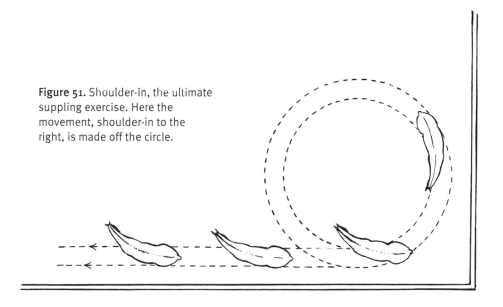

the track. The outside leg is held flat behind the girth (position B) to prevent twisting and falling out. The rider concentrates the weight on the inside seat-bone, by stretching the leg and putting more pressure on the stirrup, without leaning to the inside.

The inside rein acts behind the withers in the *fifth rein effect*, while the outside rein opens very slightly to emphasize the required direction of the opening steps, thereafter supporting its partner in maintaining the bend in the neck. Of course, the inner hand must not cross the withers.

The Golden Rule taught by the classical schools, and sometimes inadequately or carelessly expressed in national riding manuals, is that the hips remain square with the horse's hips and the shoulders square with the horse's shoulders. *The head, however, is focused on the poll, watching the track out of the corner of the eye.*

Travers, Renvers and Half-pass

Half-pass, a movement not usually asked for until the end of the secondary schooling can be approached more easily from *travers* than otherwise.

Travers, anglicized as *head-to-the-wall* or *quarters-in*, is again approached from the circle but with the bend towards the movement (see Figure 52). It begins when neck and shoulders are parallel to the wall, the forehand then proceeds directly on the track, the quarters are held inwards and the hind legs cross. The bend is held and the rider's inside leg acts on the girth to maintain the impulsion.

Renvers, otherwise known as *tail-to-the-wall* or *quarters-out*, is the reverse movement (see Figure 52) in which the horse becomes independent of the guiding wall. Both are suppling, strengthening movements and excellent exercises in control and positioning.

In *half-pass* the horse moves obliquely forward, slightly 'bent' round the rider's inside leg and with the head bent towards the movement. From the circle the horse moves forwards and sideways, the body being as near parallel to the long side of the arena as possible. The outside legs pass and cross over the inside ones.

The rider's weight is on the inside seat-bone, the inside hand is opened a trifle, thumb pointing in the direction of the movement, and is supported by the outside rein in front of the withers and on the neck. The outside leg is

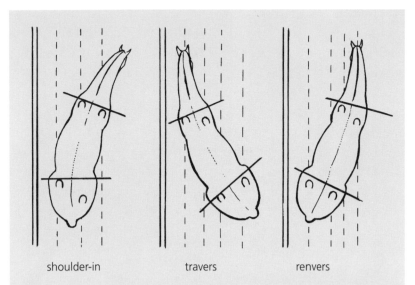

Figure 52. Comparative views of (*left*) shoulder-in; (*centre*) travers (also known as 'quarters-in' or 'head-to-the-wall'); (*right*) renvers (also known as 'tail-to-the-wall' or 'quarters-out'). All are most easily approached from the circle.

shoulder-in   travers   renvers

Half-pass to the left, horse positioned correctly immediately before outside leg crosses the inner.

179

The young chestnut horse goes one better in half-pass to the left...

and half-pass to the right, rear view.

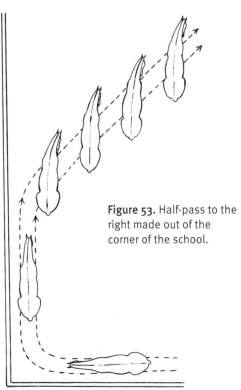

Figure 53. Half-pass to the right made out of the corner of the school.

laid flat on the girth to push the horse both sideways and forwards, while the inside leg provides the essential impulsion.

All three movements and shoulder-in are best ridden in walk before being attempted in trot.

Half-turn on the Quarters (Demi-pirouette)

This, too, belongs to the latter part of the secondary training. It is a difficult movement and should not be attempted until the horse 'carries' his head and neck (i.e. neck arched, face a little in advance of the vertical with the *poll being the highest point*). The forehand is then lightened and the horse carries the weight over his quarters.

Half-turn on the quarters (demi-pirouette).

The purpose of this important movement, completing the work begun with the forehand turn is:

1. To increase the rider's control over the quarters. In this instance the quarters have to be held in place to avoid the movement becoming no more than a turn on the centre.

2. To supple the shoulders, just as the turn on the forehand helped increase suppleness in the quarters at the opposite end.

3. To re-balance the horse by lightening the forehand just as the forehand turn lightened the quarters. Both turns are necessary to establish an overall balance.

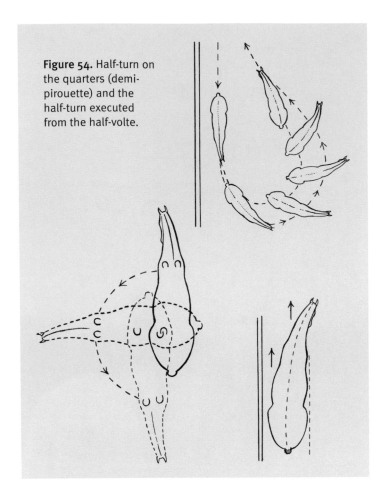

Figure 54. Half-turn on the quarters (demi-pirouette) and the half-turn executed from the half-volte.

Aids

The turn is preceded by a couple of discreet half-halts made in a good, established walk.

To turn from left to right, the right rein opens to lead the horse round, meanwhile, the left rein is laid against the neck to limit the bend of the neck and to put a check on too much movement to the front. Both hands are carried to the right (but *not* across the withers). The left leg prevents the quarters from slipping out to the side while the right controls the turn and, with a little help from its partner, provides the impulsion which is, as always, absolutely necessary. The most powerful aid, however, is when the rider places the weight on the *outside* seat-bone so as to push the horse over in the required direction.

The ideal is for the forefeet and the outside hind foot to move on the pivot of the inside hind leg.

A useful approach to the turn and one easily understood by the horse is to ride the *half-volte*, just as the *reversed half-volte* can be employed to facilitate the forehand turn (see Figure 49, page 174). The half-volte can be decreased progressively in size until, willy-nilly, it becomes a turn on the quarters and does so without endangering the forward impulse.

A useful suppling exercise to employ along with the lateral work confirming the horse in the correct directional bend.

Rein-back

Of all the movements in the equestrian compendium none is more misunderstood and none so badly performed.

The young horse is prepared to move backwards in the stable and in hand but, before the rein-back is asked for under saddle, the square halt has to be established, he needs to be put on the bit and to be sufficiently developed physically.

The aids for rein-back are as follows:

1. Ride the horse into a square halt, on the bit with poll and lower jaw relaxed – those are the prerequisites for the movement.

2. Apply both legs to ask for walk. As the horse responds the hands close on the reins (the direct rein of opposition) without any suspicion of a backward pull. The seat is lightened by a slight forward inclination of the trunk and the leg aid is reduced momentarily, then as the horse steps back the legs remain quietly in place ready to counter any deviation from the straight, two-time rein-back.

3. After two or three steps the legs are again applied and the hands open to permit the horse to move off in walk.

To help the horse the assistant can encourage him to move back by lightly tapping his front and using the voice (an aid which the rider may also use to advantage).

The rein-back is not a walk backwards. It employs diagonal limbs in a two-beat time, i.e. left fore and right hind and vice versa.

The rein-back in correct two-time.

Hacking

While the school work is of obvious importance the daily hacking session is just as much so. For both horse and rider it is certainly more enjoyable to ride out in company but towards the end of the secondary schooling it should also be possible to go out on one's own. However, whether riding singly or in company, tell someone at home where you are going and when you think you will be back. In addition, take with you a mobile phone.

Traffic Exposure

While the older horse has so far acted as a shield from traffic for his younger companion, it is now time to reduce the latter's reliance on the escort horse.

Continue to ride the youngster on the inside of the older horse but gradually encourage him, on a suitable piece of road where you can see for some distance in front, to take the lead by about a neck's distance as a vehicle approaches from the front. By degrees the distance can be increased until the two horses are in single file. When a vehicle approaches from behind, let the youngster drop back in the same way.

The advantage of riding a schooled horse in traffic conditions is that he can be positioned according to the need of the moment quietly, quickly and effectively. The ability to position the horse coupled with the habit of intelligent anticipation are prerequisites to riding safely. Indeed, the practice of riding in one's mind 100 metres in front and behind is as great a safety factor as the fluorescent clothing which attracts the attention of vehicle drivers.

To be able to leg-yield at will is an obvious advantage but nothing is so effective as the application of a little shoulder-in. Not only does it assert the rider's authority, commanding the horse's attention, but it is invaluable in placing the horse in a position of safety. It is a natural reaction to turn the horse's head away from approaching traffic but it is not a rational one. It is far better to bend the head slightly towards the traffic hazard, as in the manner of shoulder-in, which will prevent his swinging his quarters round into the path of the vehicle. Should he then shy he will do so *away* from the vehicle and into the side of the road.

Road-riding is never going to be safe, but it will be made far safer if we are riding a schooled horse who is instinctively obedient to the aids.

Canter and Gallop

Safety is one thing, but we have also to remember that hacking should be an enjoyable experience for the horse and one to which he looks forward. In the equestrian world of the twenty-first century it is all too easy to become too earnest, even to be a shade dogmatic, and for us to lose the precious element of having fun as a result.

Put your leathers up a hole or two and let the horse canter on and learn, too, how to gallop.

Young horses do need to learn how to gallop and to spend all the time going round in circles is not the way. To gallop, the horse has to lower the body mass if he is to be able to stretch out and cover the ground. In fact, a great many riders also need to learn how to gallop. There is a knack to holding and balancing a big, strong forward-going horse without hauling and pulling or even clenching the fist. The only way to acquire the knack, and experience the horse's most elemental gait, is to pull up your leathers, forget the 'sit-up, sit-down, do this, do that' of the school arena and let him go.

Introducing Water

Horses, like most animals, are able to swim without taking lessons at the local pool, but most of them, if not all, treat water with suspicion. In fact, it is not the water that alarms them but the prospect of a less than firm footing in which they might sink. Horses in the wild will instinctively avoid boggy ground, sensing its potential danger, and the fear remains with them in the domestic state.

Since water is a commonplace hazard in cross-country riding it is only sensible for us to familiarize the horse with water obstacles and to teach him how to deal with them.

Washing down the legs with a hose is a start in the familiarization process and walking through puddles, rather than curtseying round the edges of them, is another.

Somewhere on or near the hacking routes there will be a stream or a shallow rivulet with sound footing. Seek it out and encourage the horse to cross it, taking a lead from his older companion. If he objects, avoid fighting with him, although it is permissible enough to remind him of the principles of forward movement with an immediate sharp tap from the whip. In a stand-up fight, which is to be avoided, you may win the immediate battle, but the horse will remember what he regards as punishment and will forever associate it with the water. It is far more effective to dismount, get into the water yourself and lead him over. (The procedure will, of course, be made more comfortable if you have had the foresight to wear waterproof boots.) Once he is committed to the water, get him to stand for a moment or two, while you 'make much' of him.

(The army mounted formations, far better horsemasters than civilians give them credit for – and far better than the average civilian – always employed the command, 'Make much of your horses', before giving the order to dismiss – a very good precept, indeed.)

Entry into water can be made even easier by the judicious employment of 'Professor' Galvayne's harness (see Part 2 – Additional Training Aids) adapted to the circumstance. Unless you can rig a tail rope that can be operated from the saddle, which is not impossible, you will still get your feet wet, but the horse will cross the water.

Obviously, the more frequently the horse crosses or enters water the sooner he will come to regard it as a matter of course and will, in due time, make no objection to jumping in and out of water over a small log.

The Double Bridle

In the school context the purpose of the double bridle is to establish the raised head carriage, thus increasing the rider's control, lightening the forehand and contributing to an improved balance and outline.

Up to World War II and perhaps for a few years after, the emphasis in bitting and schooling lay firmly with the double bridle in one or other of its variations. Training was based on preparing the horse, through the medium of the snaffle, or even, perhaps, a bit like the Rugby Pelham, for the double bridle, which was regarded as the hallmark of the schooled horse.

(Earlier in equestrian history the classical schools of the Renaissance prepared the horse for the curb bit through the powerful nose cavesson, and Western riding to this day does the same thing with the hackamore. The origin of Western-style riding can be traced to the Spanish conquests of the sixteenth and seventeenth centuries and particularly to the Spanish settlers who created the huge ranching industry. They brought with them their own horse culture in which the horse was 'mouthed' via the nose, control being passed gradually from the noseband to the curb bit until the horse can be ridden on a floating rein in which the philosophy of 'contact' is noticeably absent.)

Today's riding is concentrated on the snaffle and a noseband of one pattern or another that closes the mouth and as nearly as possible prevents evasions of the bit's action. Some horses – one suspects most of them – may never wear a double bridle in their lives and their riders may never have used one.

For those reasons, if it is considered that the double bridle should form part of the schooling progression, there will be criteria to meet. Clearly, the rider should be knowledgeable about the purpose and action of the bridle and should be commensurately skilful in its operation. Only a rider who has learned the knack (or art) of handling the two reins independently, even when riding with both reins held in one hand, can be considered competent to teach the horse to accept and respond to the action of the bit and bradoon.

Choice of Bit and Bradoon

Bearing that in mind, a bit and bradoon need to be selected that are most suitable to the conformation of the horse's mouth. There are horses who find work in the double bridle difficult on account of their particular conformation. Horses who are thick through the jowl have problems with flexing at the poll for the very understandable reason that it causes them discomfort. Short-jawed, thickset cobby sorts may just be physically unable to accept two bits in the mouth and are really far better suited to a Pelham, though again it needs to be chosen with care. A ported mouthpiece will usually give a better result than a plain bar or mullen mouth, but the best is probably the Rugby Pelham with, of course, the ported mouthpiece.

Horses inclining more towards the Thoroughbred type are usually the best suited to a double bridle. They have naturally long jaws which accommodate the bits easily but they will rarely go as well in a Pelham since the mouthpiece has to be positioned higher than the curb groove. Inevitably, the curb chain will then rise out of the groove (lipstrap not withstanding) and will act on the jaw-bones when the curb rein is operated.

After that the bridle has to be fitted accurately and with attention being given to every detail of its adjustment. (The subject is covered comprehensively in *The Complete Book of Bitting* (David & Charles) and in *Bitting* (J.A. Allen). Modesty prevents my mentioning the author's name.)

My own preference is for a short, fixed-cheek bit of medium weight. Some very good ones are made in Germany or are marketed from that country, but, in my view, the mouthpieces incline towards being over-thick. They are made so, one imagines, in a laudable attempt to provide a broad bearing surface and reduce the potential severity of the action. In practice, however, they can be too bulky. I also find them insufficiently direct in their action as a result and thus they reduce the degree of finesse of which the bridle is capable.

The best bridlework is without doubt that of the English bridle makers, who have devoted a lot of time to designing a bridle which is broad and soft enough over the headpiece to reduce the inevitable pressure put on the poll.

Action and Purpose

In simple terms the bradoon, fitted above the curb bit in the mouth, acts on the corners to *raise* the head. The curb, when it assumes an angle of 45 degrees or more in response to rein pressure, acts upon three parts of the head causing it to be *lowered*. Used judiciously in concert with the bradoon it suggests a flexion at the poll (the highest part of the neck) and in the *lower jaw* via the agency of the curb chain, which also encourages, with the mouthpiece, a *retraction* of the nose.

The tongue port in the centre of the mouthpiece allows the tongue to be drawn into the declivity provided and so prevents it from lying over the bars of the mouth, in this way ensuring that the mouthpiece on either side of the port is in direct contact the them (the bars are that area of gum between the incisor and molar teeth).

The action of the mouthpiece is then downward and slightly to the rear. In turn that is assisted by the curb chain tightening in the *curb groove* as the eye of the bit, to which it is attached, moves forward. The head position comes about, therefore, by the lowering of the head, the flexion of the poll and lower jaw and the subsequent retraction of the nose, the whole being balanced by the lifting action of the bradoon.

The lowering influence is assisted by pressure being applied at the *poll* as the eye of the bit moves forward on its permitted arc and transmits a downward pressure via the cheekpieces to the bridle headpiece. (The longer the cheek above the mouthpiece, the greater the poll pressure that can be employed.)

We know that the outline of the horse is governed by the delicate balance between the driving legs at the girth and the restraining action of the hands on the mouth. Similarly, *the carriage of the head is obtained and governed by the hands balancing the raising effect of the bradoon with the lowering effect of the curb. That is, indeed, a matter of finesse.*

The curb chain is a component crucial to the success of the bridle. Fitted snugly, but obviously not too tight, it will act as the eye of the bit approaches the 45 degree position in response to very light rein pressure. Fitted too loosely, in a mistaken act of kindness, the whole action becomes commensurately more severe since the action is delayed until the eye is well past the 45 degree optimum position. Moreover, in that situation, the curb chain rises out of the curb groove to chafe the unprotected jaw-bones. This failing is encouraged and the chafing accentuated because of the current fashion to dispense with the *lipstrap*, which used to be thought integral to the bridle. Its purpose was to hold the curb chain in the curb groove. Without it, the chain is likely to ride upwards to bear on the thinly covered jaw-bones, a tendency accentuated if it is adjusted loosely.

First Steps

Fit the bridle in the stable, making sure that, while the curb bit fits snugly and rests centrally over the bars, the eyes of the bit incline sufficiently outwards, away from the face, so that there is no risk of chafing. Use either a double-link curb chain or, better still, one made from soft leather or elastic. If a metal chain is used it is advisable to encase it in a rubber guard.

When the bridle is fitting *perfectly* put a small feed in the manger and let the horse eat it while still wearing his bridle. In order to eat it is necessary for the lower jaw to be relaxed, which is the first lesson the young horse has to learn.

Carry out this procedure for three or four days, which will allow the horse to become familiar with the feeling of the bits in his mouth.

The next lesson is to bridle the horse and then to position him with his quarters into a corner so that he cannot draw back when we begin to manipulate the bits. Pass the reins over the horse's head, taking the bradoon rein in the left hand, holding it some 25 cm (10 in) from the bit rings and above the nose. Hold the curb rein in the right hand, the same distance from the bit, but behind the horse's chin.

Now the head can be raised two or three times by the fingers vibrating on the bradoon, then the curb rein can be applied in the same way to get the horse to drop his nose and relax the lower jaw. Practise the two actions separately, *yielding the rein the moment the horse yields*, and be content with just a little at this stage.

If the horse resists the movement of the curb by a muscular contraction, counteract by using the bradoon rein.

When the horse understands the pressures exerted by both, and responds to them, go a step further and get him to accept alternate pressures made by the two hands.

That accomplished, and it will not take more than a day or two, take the horse into the school and, facing the rear, hold the reins in the manner described. Then persuade the horse to walk forwards while you, of course, walk backwards.

The whole essence of the exercise is in the horse moving forward confidently, going into the hands and not holding back from them. To ensure free, forward movement (FFM) the assistant must be in attendance to follow up and encourage the horse to advance. Once the horse is walking freely the flexion exercises can be carried out as before but with the difference of the horse being in movement.

Finally, the reins are returned to their proper place and the trainer, standing a little in advance of the nearside shoulder and facing forwards, can hold the bradoon rein in the right hand and the curb in the left, both hands being, of course, behind the horse's head and held at approximately the same height as they would be with a rider in the saddle. The head can be raised a little with the bradoon and then the trainer can ask, by a manipulation of the fingers, for the horse to flex to the right and to the left.

When this can be accomplished easily at halt it can be practised at the walk, with the assistant following up as before. The direction can then be altered from side to side according to which flexion is being applied, resistance being corrected with the bradoon rein.

Within a week the horse should be able to circle the school to either hand and be flexing correctly and may even be able to describe a zigzag.

The horse is then ready to be ridden in the bridle at walk and, since he is now familiar with its actions, neither he nor his rider should experience any untoward difficulties. Initially, however, the rider will need to apply active legs to push the horse always into his bridle and should delay asking for trot and canter work for some days.

The Rein in the Hand

To help the rider differentiate between the two reins it is usual for the bradoon rein to be broader than the curb, but the manner in which they are held varies according to the school of thought or, perhaps, the national practice.

In Britain the bradoon rein is most frequently held outside the little finger and outside the curb rein, which is held between the third and fourth finger. In this position there is a little doubt that the bradoon is the predominant influence.

Held in the opposite fashion, which is the more logical since it corresponds to the position of the bits in the mouth, the tendency is for the curb to predominate. In this second instance the bradoon is brought into play by the hands being turned a little upwards in a lifting action to raise the head, and downwards when one wants to lower it.

The middle way is to hold the bradoon rein outside the little finger, but with the end of the curb rein leaving the hand through the *first and second fingers*, the bradoon end being passed over the first finger and being held in place by the thumb. The latter stops the bradoon rein slipping through the hand, while the two middle fingers act easily to increase or release pressure on the curb rein. This does require dexterity and a deal of practise, but then so do the finger exercises on the piano!

Jumping

The foundation of the jumping exercises is the work on the flat, which prepares the horse in the best possible way.

The exercises and movements on the flat develop and supple the horse and improve his balance. Moreover, they act positively to increase the rider's control, ensuring willing obedience and submission. Put together, these factors contribute to the horse's gymnastic ability and, as a result, to the level of his subsequent performance over fences.

Most horses enjoy jumping and, I think, regard it as a mental relaxation after the frequently demanding school work. *They stop finding it fun if they are over-faced or over-jumped.* However, not all of them have a talent for jumping and there are always the occasional ones who are less than enthusiastic about leaving the ground. Nevertheless, the majority can be encouraged by progressive exercises to jump fences reliably up to 1.2 m (4 ft) in height and/or width.

Developing Jumping on the Lunge

As described at an earlier stage, jumping on the lunge is a good introduction to jumping under saddle. It allows the horse to adjust his balance and stride on his own initiative without the distraction of the rider's weight and, sometimes, hands.

The objective is to have the horse operating fluently over an upright fence of about 90 cm (3 ft) and over a spread fence of the same height and with an average spread of 1.2 m (4 ft) in the course of a few lessons. The spread fence does not need to be a true parallel, which is more difficult for the inexperienced horse to negotiate, but can be built so that the second element is 15 cm (6 in) higher than the first to give something of a *staircase* effect.

To help the horse acquire technique and a degree of self-initiative, too, fences should be given a ground-line and be preceded by a distance pole – a most invaluable jumping aid – placed 3 m (10 ft) in front of the fence. The distance pole helps the horse to judge the approach and take-off and discourages any tendency to rush.

The fences, placed for convenience on each long side, should be jumped from both directions, altering the staircase construction accordingly, and out of trot. On landing the horse may make a few strides at canter, which is natural enough, but he must then be asked to return to trot and then to walk before he jumps another fence. Jumping is exciting and requiring the horse to return to a slower gait is a way of imposing discipline and containing the excitement element within reasonable bounds.

Lunge jumping is beneficial in every way but the success of the exercises depends a lot on the trainer's competence and ability to present the horse at the fence to best advantage. The fence has to be jumped from a straight approach with the horse being allowed to continue for a few strides on the same line after landing. If the horse has to jump on the arc of a circle with his head and neck inclined toward the trainer by reason of the rein, he can easily get into the undesirable habit of jumping to the left or right. The secret is in moving parallel to the horse, only asking for him to resume the circle a few strides after landing.

(Later in the ridden training there are strengthening exercises involving jumping on the circle that are also designed to improve accuracy and balance, but they are best excluded from the lunge work.)

Phases of the Jump

Lunge jumping gives the rider/trainer an opportunity to study the attitude of the horse in the different phases of the jump.

1. *Take-off*

2. *Flight*

3. *Landing*

To which may be added at either end of the spectrum the approach and getaway strides.

The lesson to be learned from observing the horse jumping without the inhibition of the rider's weight is this: *If the rider sits in balance with the horse throughout the phases of the jump and in no way attempts to interfere with the movement, the outline in each phase should not differ from that assumed when the horse is jumping free.*

Approach
Correctly presented at the fence and ridden with minimal interference, the horse raises the head in the approach so as to focus on the fence and judge his take-off. The hind legs are almost simultaneously brought further under the body preparatory to entering the take-off phase.

Take-off

At the point of take-off, head and neck are raised and the forelegs act to lift up the forehand. The engaged quarters then thrust powerfully upwards to propel the body into the flight phase.

Flight

Head and neck are extended and the forelegs tucked up. Simultaneously, the horse begins to form an arc over the highest point of the fence, rounding the back and stretching forward the head and neck. The word used to describe this attitude is the French *bascule*.

Landing

The forelegs are outstretched and the feet touch the ground *one after another*, the horse carrying his weight on one foot for a split second. To adjust the balance by re-distributing the weight (which at the moment of landing is concentrated over the forehand), the head and neck, as the balancing agents for the body mass, are raised. They are lowered when the hind legs touch down and the horse goes into the *getaway* stride.

Interference from the rider, whether voluntary or involuntary, has an immediate adverse effect on the outline that may cause the fence to be hit and is likely to subject the animal to additional strain; nor, of course, is it calculated to do much for his confidence and enjoyment of the exercises.

Loose Schooling

Working the horse loose is an extension of the lunge exercises. The latter allowed for control and the imposition of a jumping discipline; loose schooling over fences goes a stage further and is even more beneficial. It teaches the horse to judge a fence on his own account, with or without a distance pole; it encourages his initiative and is a great confidence-booster. Moreover, the horse clearly enjoys the freedom integral to the work.

Loose schooling also emphasizes the value of teaching the horse obedience to the voice. When first loosed into the school area he is, admittedly, likely to be deaf to the voice but, having let off steam with a buck and a kick, he will begin to respond.

The fences used in loose schooling may include all four basic types i.e. *upright, staircase, parallel* and *pyramid* (see Fence Variety, page 202) and can certainly, as the horse becomes more experienced, be as much as 90 cm (3 ft) or even 15 cm (6 in) higher than that, while the spreads can be 1.2 m (4 ft) in width.

Working the horse loose allows him to relax mentally and physically and encourages free movement.

Jumping loose over a variety of fences is, of course, an excellent preparation for jumping them with the rider on board, although at the outset it is only sensible to reduce the size until the horse is confident in himself *and his rider*.

Jumping loose adds a fun element to the training and horses seem to enjoy the exercise. Importantly, it also encourages initiative, balance and judgement of the approach.

Mounted Jumping

Jumping in the secondary stage is first concerned with recapitulating the work done in the primary schooling, particularly over the grid, and can then be extended into more ambitious exercises.

Simple Combinations

The first combination fence is approached out of the corner either over a three-pole grid or a distance pole leading to a straightforward cross-pole fence (this is the easiest schooling fence that can be employed, since its construction persuades the horse to jump specifically across its centre, the lowest point in the fence). The second fence, a small spread, is placed 5.5 m (18 ft) from the first. Initially, the height of both need not exceed 60 cm (2 ft) and the spread on the latter 1.2 m (4 ft) in width.

The distance (5.5 m – 18 ft) between the elements allows the horse one non-jumping stride between the two fences, i.e. between landing over the first and the take-off point for the second. The average canter stride for a horse is between 3.3 m and 3.6 m (11–12 ft) and becomes longer as the speed increases. The optimum point of take-off at this height approximates to the height of the fence; at a 1.2 m (4 ft) fence the optimum take-off point is about one-and-a-third times the height.

To ride this simple combination involves the rider applying the leg aid to jump the first element and then again on landing. The horse takes one stride and the legs are again applied decisively to ask for the take-off over the second element. They act once more on landing to prevent any tendency for the horse to 'dwell' in the getaway stride. The rider must always ride away from the fence before, in this instance, returning the horse to trot from canter.

A balanced approach to the fence with the seat in light contact.

Using a distance pole to help the horse over the first small cross-pole fence.

Jumping a low pole as part of a sequence of small fences.

As an extension of the one-stride combination, a parallel or pyramid-type fence can be added 10 m (33 ft) from the second element. This distance allows for two non-jumping strides and calls for concentration by both partners, the rider being quite clear about the leg aids that will need to be applied. The one-stride distance calls for the legs to be applied twice – once on landing over the first element and once more to ask for take-off over the second. Two strides between the second and third elements require the aids to act with increasing definition three times, the final squeeze asking for take-off.

Distance Poles and Ground-lines

So far, the distance poles and the correct siting of the schooling fences have helped the horse to arrive correctly at the point of take-off. The next stage is to remove that dependence and encourage the horse to work out the problems for himself – with, of course, a little help from his rider.

The poles can still be retained but the distances can be varied to give one, two or three non-jumping strides (13.5 m – 44 ft) when the approach is made in canter.

The ground-pole placed in front of the fence can also be dispensed with, so long as the fence is constructed to afford an in-built ground-line.

Alternatively, ground-poles can be used to correct or even impose the trajectory of the leap. Used with a distance pole placed to give three non-jumping strides, or, indeed, with no distance pole at all, the horse can be encouraged to stand-off the fence, involving greater effort, by moving the pole further away from the base. Conversely, a ground-pole close up to the fence encourages the horse to 'go in deep' to make the leap and to increase the arc of the bascule.

Changes of Direction

Jumping single fences is relatively straightforward; jumping which calls for precisely executed changes of direction is more complex and puts a premium on approach, impulsion and balance. The ideal exercise is to jump fences placed on a figure-of-eight.

Initially, the fences should be kept low and should be preceded by one-stride distance poles, which can be varied to give one, two, three or four non-jumping strides as the exercise progresses. The figure is ridden (see Figure 55) at trot round the short sides, and at canter on the diagonals.

The exercise acts as a lead-in to the change of direction and leg at the canter.

Before attempting the figure-of-eight over fences it is advisable, using some strategically placed markers, to practise riding the figure very accurately at trot while maintaining impulsion and rhythm.

Angled Fences

Jumping at an angle is one of the basic exercises. It teaches accuracy and obedience and is the lead-in to changing the leading leg virtually in mid-air – often a necessary accomplishment when jumping an arena course.

Jumping from an angle, across the obstacle, does, of course, increase the possibility of an unsteady horse running out and down the line of the fence.

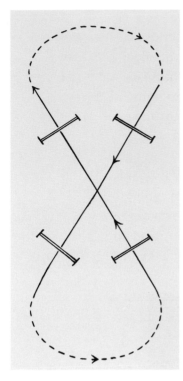

Figure 55. An exercise in making changes of direction. The broken line is executed at trot, the approach across the diagonal at canter.

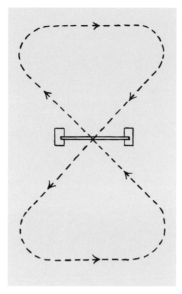

Figure 56. A simple exercise over a low fence used to teach the horse to jump at an angle.

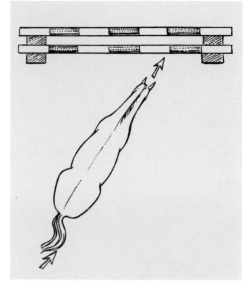

Figure 57. Following a run-out to the left the approach is made at an angle to the right.

Approaching from the left the horse can run out to the right along the obstacle and vice versa. It demands, therefore, concentration on the part of the rider and obedience and some initiative from the horse.

The fence is built initially in the centre of the arena and is ridden from a figure-of-eight. It need not exceed 75 cm (2 ft 6 in) in height.

The fence should first be jumped at trot until the exercise can be performed with complete accuracy. Thereafter, it can be jumped from canter, returning to trot on the short sides and then striking off on the opposite canter lead as the approach is made off the opposite diagonal.

Bounce Fences, Grids and Poles

A 'bounce' fence is a combination allowing no stride at all between the elements. Its purpose is to increase suppleness and gymnastic ability and, along with the grid, it is a very useful strengthening exercise.

As an introduction use two small fences 3.6 m (12 ft) apart with a

Turns and corners:

right Exercise of jumping a 'Vee'-fence on a circle. On landing the horse is turned right to jump the fence in the background.

centre A useful 'Vee'-fence exercise that demands accuracy.

bottom Jumping the corner, another exercise in obedience and accuracy.

distance pole placed at 5.5 m (18 ft) from the combination. It is best approached initially at a good, strong trot. The rider's legs are applied firmly on landing over the first element and the horse is left with no alternative other than to 'bounce' over the second.

Bounce fences, for the sake of variety, can be incorporated into a combination of related fences, i.e. one might commence with an upright followed by the bounce combination two non-jumping strides away and then by another obstacle placed one or two non-jumping strides further on.

A fun training aid, much enjoyed by horses and riders, and greatly beneficial to both, is the jumping grid. It is a line of up to six low, fixed fences 45 cm (18 in) high and placed at the bounce distance (3.6 m – 12 ft) apart and, if possible, enclosed by a rail. It is ridden at canter and for the rider is in the nature of an enjoyable switchback ride.

Tackling a small bounce fence preceded by a distance pole.

Jumping the first element of a combination in the sequence of small, varied fences.

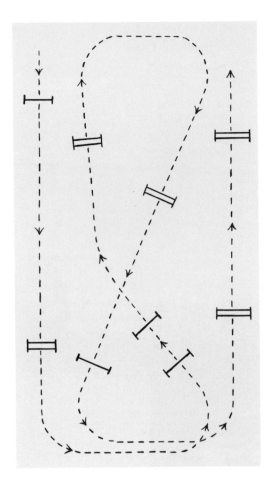

Figure 58. A simple, easily erected practice course.

There are a number of other useful exercises, one of particular value being the 'pen' complex. In its simplest form this is a rectangle of low uprights which can be jumped in and out on a bounce distance or, using the longer stride, as a one-stride combination. It can, also, if room allows, be jumped on the diagonal, or one can jump in, halt and turn before jumping out. A 'farmyard' complex is a bigger and altogether more ambitious structure, comprising a square of different fences – rails, banks, brush, wall etc., thus offering a variety of choices when it comes to jumping in and out.

Fence Variety

Upright, staircase, parallel and pyramid fences are all included in the horse's training since they present different problems in respect of take-offs and angles of descent. The take-off zone for an *upright* fence of average size is between a distance equal to the height of the fence and up to one and one-third times its height – the latter being closer to the optimum than otherwise.

For the fence to be jumped successfully the point of take-off and landing should be equidistant from the bottom of the fence. The horse should reach the highest point of the arc made when jumping the fence when he is directly over the top of the obstacle.

In fact, the *upright* fence is the most difficult of all to jump since if the horse takes off too close he will hit the fence on the way up, whereas if he stands off too far he is likely to hit it with the hind legs on his way down – hence the use of the ground- pole in the training. Placed at the appropriate distance in relation to the fence's height it is used to produce a correct take-off, while a further pole placed at a similar distance on the landing side will control the angle of descent should it become too steep, as the horse will reach out to clear it.

A *staircase* is a much easier and more encouraging obstacle than an upright. It is a fence built with two or three bars at ascending heights, as in the case of a triple bar obstacle, and its shape corresponds to the parabola of the leap. The highest point of the leap will be in line with the highest element in the fence and occurs in the middle of the flight phase.

The horse lands well out from the fence and the angle of descent is less steep than in the case of an upright obstacle. In consequence the getaway stride is relatively long in comparison with the shorter stride following an upright.

It is very necessary that these factors should be understood and taken into account when estimating distances between combination fences.

Parallel fences comprise two elements which, in a true parallel, are of the same height. Lowering the first element introduces a staircase quality and makes the jump easier.

It is often thought that a parallel causes the horse to take-off well away from it and, indeed, this is the usual reaction of the unschooled horse. However, this involves a very big effort, often accompanied by a decrease in accuracy.

The most successful way of tackling a parallel is to make the take-off closer to the fence than would be advisable when jumping an upright. The reason is because the horse has to reach the highest point of the leap when he is closer to the rear bar than the one in the front of the fence. In consequence his landing is well out from the fence and because the angle of descent is less abrupt the getaway stride is longer.

A small spread fence encourages scope and the ability to stretch over parallels.

A *pyramid* fence comprises three elements, the first and last of equal heights and the central one higher. It can, of course, be jumped from both directions but it needs to be constructed carefully and be neither too high nor with too great a spread, since the horse does not see the final element and could suffer injury as a result of attempting to jump the obstacle. It is, nonetheless, looked upon as being within the spread fence category and again the getaway stride will be longer than that from an upright.

Use of poles to maintain straightness:

right Poles placed on the ground to encourage straightness through grids/combinations and

below The landing made accurately through the straightening poles.

More advanced exercises.

above A more difficult exercise in jumping off a circle over a higher fence. It requires accuracy, obedience and agility, as well as riding ability.

left The horse is halted in the approach to the fence in a lesson of obedience which checks any tendency to rush.

Distances

The distance in combination fences is a crucial factor. When building combination fences of 1.2 m (4 ft) in height and with that spread, the following distances allow for the differences in the angle of descent and their effect on the length of the getaway stride. They are based on an average canter stride of 3.3–3.6 m (11–12 ft)

Upright to Upright	7.3 m (24 ft) one non-jumping stride
	10–10.7 m (33–35 ft) two non-jumping strides
Upright to Spread	7.0 m (23 ft) one non-jumping stride
	9.75–10.0 m (32–33 ft) two non-jumping strides
Spread to Upright	7.6 m (25 ft) one non-jumping stride
	10.0–10.7 m (33–35 ft) two non-jumping strides
Spread to Spread	7.3 m (24 ft) one non-jumping stride
	10–10.7 m (33–35 ft) two non-jumping strides

(The same formula is applied to three non-jumping strides 13.5 m (44 ft); four 16.8 m (55 ft) and five 20 m (66 ft), the addition or subtraction of 0.3 m (1 ft) between types of fences being the same.)

Fences are *related* between 11.9 m and 24 m (39 ft and 79 ft) apart; below 11.6 m (38 ft) they become combinations.

Refusals

In a perfect world there would be no acknowledgement of the possibility of refusals. In the real world they do occur, however carefully planned and executed the training programme, and we need to deal with them appropriately as they arise, while being aware of the principal reasons that may cause horses to stop at fences.

Horses may refuse, or even stop jumping until the source of their action is recognized and addressed, because:

1. They are being *over-faced* by the fence being too big, or because they lack the experience to tackle it successfully. Or because they have been *over-jumped* and become sickened with the whole business.

2. They may be feeling discomfort from having jarred their legs or from a strained back or pulled muscle. Horses who have been made to jump

when suffering from soreness of this nature may refuse long after the trouble has cleared up.

3. They stop if the act of jumping causes pain, which is understandable. A common source of pain is an ill-fitting saddle that pinches as the back is arched over the fence and, of course, the less than competent rider who jabs the mouth on take-off. A bad experience at a fence that is either painful or frightening, or both, will diminish confidence and can be long-lasting in its effect.

4. Rider error is one of the most common sources of refusals. A principal failing is the laudable concern with not getting behind the movement which causes a rider to get *in front of the movement* in the approach, losing contact with the mouth and over-weighting the forehand. Flailing legs contribute to an increase in speed and a commensurate loss of balance and the horse, displaying more sense than his rider, slides into a determined stop. Speed only flattens the trajectory of the leap. The ideal jump is made from impulsion out of a state of balance.

5. Horses stop or run-out if they find themselves wrong at a fence, usually through no fault of their own. In doing so they display their good sense.

Since the act of jumping is never going to be an exact science, there will be the occasional stop or run-out with the best of horses and riders, although it is equally true that the chances of a refusal are much reduced by good basic training and competent riding.

When it happens, don't panic. Instead, in the event of a run-out, circle quietly but swiftly in the *opposite* direction, turn in off the circle and present the horse to the fence at a slight angle from the side to which he ran out. That is, if he went out to the left bring him in from the left, which makes it nearly impossible for him to run out to the same side again. Take care, however, that the angle of approach is not too shallow, otherwise you are inviting him to run out across the front of the fence.

In training, whether the horse stops dead or runs out, have the fence lowered and jump it at the lower height for the next day or two before raising it again – assuming that it was not impossibly high in the first place.

Jumping Frequency

The surest way to stop the horse jumping freely and enjoying himself over fences is to jump too much. It is sufficient to have a short, well-planned jumping session once or twice a week. As the training progresses more demanding fences and combinations can be introduced and in the latter part of the four-year-old programme one or two big fences can be jumped just once during the week.

Cross-country

Riding cross-country is an altogether more rumbustious affair than arena jumping, which is more disciplined and precise. Both horse and rider have to adjust their technique to account for the far greater emphasis given to the approach because of the variety of terrain involved. Nonetheless, the school jumping exercises are an essential preparation for riding outside the restrictions imposed by the 'long' and 'short' sides of the arena.

The essence of cross-country riding is:

1. To accustom the horse to cope with natural terrain and the continual alterations in balance made necessary by going up and down hills while maintaining an easy, economical *rhythm*.

2. To ride over low, fixed fences and natural obstacles, like banks, water, ditches, etc., and for them to be jumped with minimal rider intervention out of the horse's natural stride.

The gait to adopt is a good, swinging canter in the rhythm and cruising speed that are natural to the horse. The rider's concern is to sit in balance while keeping a steady contact with legs and hands.

However, there is a noticeable difference between riding in the school area and in the outdoor environment. In general, or even simple, terms, horses in the school, going nowhere other than in circles, tend to need active legs to maintain impulsion. Outdoors, the natural impulsion increases and the emphasis shifts more towards the restraining aids of hand and body-weight.

In short, the horse may take a stronger hold and that, within reason, is to be encouraged. However, there will be occasions when the enthusiasm needs to be checked and this is best accomplished by the hands acting alternately or by fixing one hand at the withers and acting with the other against the base which it provides.

Riding *uphill* the horse has to be able to employ the propulsive force of the quarters and so the rider needs to fold the upper body forward from the hips to allow them full freedom. Meanwhile the hands have to allow extension of the neck without loss of contact.

above Jumping off a bank that is typical of the cross-country course. Horse and rider are in harmony and in excellent balance.

Cross-country schooling; an exemplary picture of a confident combination.

Going *downhill* is not so easy and steep slopes need to be preceded by work on more gentle inclines. Downhill slopes can be ridden first at walk with the rider's legs insisting that the horse moves forward steadily and *straight*. If the quarters swing out so that the horse is across the slope there is a real danger of his legs slipping from under him. Any tendency to hurry should be countered by the fingers closing intermittently on the reins. Indeed, contact has to be maintained throughout since it allows the horse to relate his balance to a still, central point.

The true follower of Caprilli will incline the trunk forward, but it should certainly not be carried so far forward as to over-weight the forehand and encourage the horse to increase the speed of the descent in order to keep his balance. Nor, of course, must the rider sit back and in opposite fashion over-weight the quarters and prevent the hind legs from being well engaged under the body. As in all things, moderation is the key. Indeed, moderation combined with reasonable prudence and the ability to adapt to the given circumstance is the secret of cross-country riding.

In general, it is advisable for the rider to adopt a less than forward position over cross-country fences. The Weedon-trained horseman of the British army called it a 'balanced seat' and over drop fences they would most certainly have held the body in the vertical plane, 'slipping' the rein as necessary, which is the course followed by the modern event rider.

At the present time, hunting in Britain as we know it may no longer be an option and we are, therefore, denied the best schooling ground for the cross-country horse. Drag-hunting can become too hairy and too exciting for young horses and is not an entirely feasible option. Nonetheless, cross-country rides in company, or the occasional visit to a well-built, artificial course, with easier options available for the beginner, are good alternatives.

Where Now?

In the human context the secondary education of the pupil attaining the prescribed levels is followed by further 'university' education, and it is there that the analogy between the human and equine systems parts company.

Very few horses go further than the secondary stage (while some never complete anything in advance of a superficial primary schooling). However, having completed the secondary education the gifted horse *can* specialize in one or other of the major disciplines for which he appears to be best suited.

Whether he does or not depends on the dedication, talent, circumstances and, perhaps, the ambition of the owner.

To compete at the highest level it is probable that riders must turn professional but it is possible to compete at what might be termed a good 'county' level in eventing, show-jumping and dressage while still being involved with a job and family commitments.

Otherwise, if one's ambition and circumstances extend to no more than happy hacking, then one can be a very happy hacker on a schooled, well-mannered horse.

The object of this book is that stated at the outset – the production of an all-round riding horse happy and able to turn his hand, or hoof, to a variety of activities.

Index